MY NATURAL HISTORY

· · · · ·

THE *evolution* OF
A GARDENER

· · · · ·

LIZ PRIMEAU

My

NATURAL

HISTORY

GREYSTONE BOOKS
Douglas & McIntyre Publishing Group
Vancouver / Toronto / Berkeley

Greystone Books
A division of Douglas & McIntyre Ltd.
2323 Quebec Street, Suite 201
Vancouver, British Columbia
Canada v5T 4S7
www.greystonebooks.com

Library and Archives Canada Cataloguing in Publication
Primeau, Liz
My natural history / Liz Primeau.

ISBN 978-1-55365-376-9

1. Primeau, Liz. 2. Gardening—Canada. 3. Gardening—Psychological aspects.
4. Gardeners—Canada—Biography. I. Title.
SB63.P75A3 2008   635.092   C2008-903326-4

Editing by Susan Folkins
Copy editing by Iva Cheung
Jacket and text design by Jessica Sullivan
Jacket images © Veer Incorporated
Printed and bound in Canada by Friesens
Printed on acid-free paper that is forest friendly (100% post-consumer
recycled paper) and has been processed chlorine free.
Distributed in the U.S. by Publishers Group West

We gratefully acknowledge the financial support of the Canada
Council for the Arts, the British Columbia Arts Council,
the Province of British Columbia through the Book Publishing Tax Credit,
and the Government of Canada through the Book Publishing Industry
Development Program (BPIDP) for our publishing activities.

For my Dad and Uncle Ren,
who gave me the gift of good memories,
and for Chris, who
taught me how to laugh at myself.

CONTENTS

Prologue 1

· · · · ·

· · · · ·

"Green fingers are the extension of a verdant heart. A good garden cannot be made by somebody who has not developed the capacity to know and love growing things."
RUSSELL PAGE, The Education of a Gardener

. . . . .

A CERTAIN IMPORTANT person in my household said to me not long ago that what you like to do as a young person probably reflects your natural skills to a certain extent—or words to that effect. He made this comment during one of our philosophical conversations, which seem to occur on Saturday mornings during our marathon newspaper-reading sessions.

Who knows what brought it up, but as I recall we pondered further on whether you might actually be born with a talent for art or carpentry or music. We've both known families in which an ability to paint or play an instrument or even make a nice cabinet seemed to be passed along through successive generations. Then again, maybe inborn talent doesn't play a role at all—maybe your dad liked to fix engines and you developed expertise as a mechanic just because you liked to hang out with your dad as a kid. And, even with apparently inherited talent, would Mozart have become Mozart if he hadn't had a stage daddy to make sure he developed his abilities?

At that point in our discussion we realized we had entered into murky nature-versus-nurture territory; we decided that no one before us had settled the question and we weren't going to either, so we went back to our newspapers and coffee.

But the conversation stuck in my head. The phrase "green thumb"—or, in Russell Page's timeless phrase, "green fingers"—didn't enter our discussion even once, but I've often wondered what really makes a gardener and whether you might inherit a metaphorically coloured digit that urged you to grow things, just as you might inherit real webbed toes (as I did, and which, unfortunately, haven't helped me aquatically). To some, gardening is a compulsion, to the point that it feels like a genetic imperative: some gardeners are convinced they were born to garden and would do so no matter what, and I put myself in that category. When meeting people interested more in financial speculation or making a big score in a game than in the way the grass grows (unless it's on a golf course), I've sometimes wondered whether they were born to care about nature but rejected it for more worldly interests. Maybe they grew up downtown and never saw things grow; maybe their fathers read the financial pages aloud over breakfast and asked questions later. Maybe they never had the opportunity to follow their natural instincts.

I was luckier—I grew up with two gardeners, first my dad and then an uncle, which allowed me to evolve as a gardener. And in my formative years I was allowed the freedom to explore: first the prairies just outside Winnipeg, where we lived until I was in my teens, and then, after we moved to a farm in southern Ontario, the fields and streams of the rural countryside.

I would never underestimate the impact of those early experiences. But still I mulled. *There's got to be something behind the notion that people are born with green thumbs,* I said to myself, *even if that darn thumb is metaphorical.* Maybe the need to grow things had its beginning in a fundamental survival mechanism, but, like my webbed toes, its importance receded through millennia as civilization advanced. Even if it was an innate capacity, however, it would need to be cultivated. As Page says: "A good garden cannot be made by somebody who has not developed the capacity to know and love growing things."

Here's how I see the history of the green thumb, and although this account is based on my imagination and the little we know about the history of gardening before 3000 BC, I'll wager that at least part of it is true (or that at least no one can prove me wrong): Thousands and thousands of years ago, a curious and smarter-than-usual gathering woman, the distaff half of a hunting and gathering couple, having realized that the plants she'd foraged for dinner sprang forth anew from those little specks that fell to the ground from their showy parts, stopped gathering and began growing. She may not have understood plant biology, but that hardly mattered. She sensed that she no longer needed to roam, that food could be made available right outside her door. Her neighbours, marvelling at her cleverness, followed her example. Then their other halves got together and built a fence, perhaps of branches and stones, enclosing the space to protect the harvest and the group from marauding animals, and the first communal farm appeared. Natural selection over the millennia favoured the new farmers, those humans who could see the connection between the seeds and the ensuing plants and pass their knowledge down to their children, and this understanding of the plant world was eventually represented in our DNA. Or so I imagine.

Before long, maybe several thousand years later, another curious and adventurous woman—because surely it had to be a woman!—decided to plant some of those pretty flowers out in the field in the enclosure. And the idea of a pleasure garden was born.

This neolithic homemaker may have had no language to describe what she was doing, but she understood that gardens are for more than growing food, that they contribute to our well-being, and her understanding has been passed along through the generations. From the enclosed gardens of ancient Persia, through the Romans' peristyle gardens hidden behind the walls of their homes and the monastery gardens of the Middle Ages to today's fenced-in backyard patios, gardens have cooled and protected and sustained us through the centuries, as well as provided creative satisfaction and mental therapy when we needed it.

I've had three gardens in my life, each fulfilling all of the above. But none of them has dominated my life—they take their place, as all beneficial interests do. In all my gardens plants have come and gone, and in each of them I've felt both content and distraught over its appearance. Sometimes I've come to the end of the rope and just said to hell with it and looked the other way. Every year each garden has looked different, depending on both nature's and the gardener's intervention, a fact that applies to all gardens. But in all my years of gardening—decades, actually— I've realized I'm no different than other gardeners, even possibly my hypothetical neolithic woman. We all experience similar highs, similar lows. We all reject the practice at some point then adopt it again, with zest and renewed enthusiasm. It *is* an obsession, but a good one.

And here's something else I've learned, and this lesson I find more compelling than knowing that contemporary gardeners share similar traits, as do chefs or politicians: over the centuries, even over millennia, *people* haven't changed much. Maybe this is something anthropologists and sociologists already know, but human nature seems to stay the course, even after we discover the wheel and invent a printing press and make an airplane and create an Internet that connects the world. Life may become easier, but when we deal with the earth, we're essentially still neolithic man and woman. Given the opportunity to spend time in the arms of nature, all of us—not just the obsessed gardeners among us—realize we like the feel of earth sifting through our fingers, we relax with the warm sun on our backs, and the tired feeling after pruning the shrubs or building a fence is a *good* tired. Most of us learn to value decaying leaves and plants because we realize they replenish nature; we learn to love seeing things grow, to harvest the green onions and pick the sweet peas. Is this affinity for the natural world born in us?

I'll never have an answer to my question about the genetic component of gardening because science has far more compelling issues to contemplate, but this I can say with certainty because I've been there: growing things is a basic element of life, and gardening is a wise instructor in the art of living. It's a journey, not a destination, and I've taken nearly a lifetime to learn that.

❦

CHAPTER 1

Born

TO GARDEN

. . . . .

S OMEONE ONCE asked me what started me on my gardening journey, and in a nanosecond the answer came to me in wide screen: green-onion sandwiches.

I say wide screen because the question triggered a movie clip from my life—the kind we all keep stored up there in the grey matter waiting to be retrieved with the right cue—and it took up the wall-to-wall expanse of my mind's eye.

It opens with my mom and an eleven-year-old me sneaking out the kitchen door on a hot Winnipeg night, with dusk deepening the sky from lavender to grey, the birds chirping their gentle goodnights and the crickets loudly THX-ing their good mornings. (My movie clip has sound, too.)

Only the light from the big bay window in the dining room illuminates our crime: stealing green onions from my dad's vegetable patch. These we stealthily carry back to the faucet in the kitchen, where we gently wash, trim, and slice them and reverently put them between two pieces of mayonnaise-slathered white bread.

Then we down them ravenously, grinning at each other like a couple of Bugs Bunnies.

One might wonder what a fondness for green-onion sandwiches has to do with gardening, but it's perfectly logical once you think about it. I was young enough to still be fascinated by how things grew, and it was a miracle to me to give a small tug and feel the onion let go of the soft earth, then to smell its pungent aroma and know I could actually *eat* something that had spent its life in the dirt. The same went for the sweet baby carrots Mom roasted for Sunday dinner, although I hated when she referred to them as babies. The peas and beans that turned from pretty little flowers into edible green things were a wonder, too. I preferred the peas, because I could surreptitiously pick a handful and scoop them out of their pods for a playtime snack. Well, maybe not as surreptitiously as I thought.

What child is not delighted by nature's miracles, even if she doesn't think of them as miraculous? Like most kids, I liked the feel of the earth for making mudpies or miniature roads and landscapes for toy trucks. I liked its smell, too, especially after a rain. The earthworms I wasn't so sure about, but Dad told me they helped loosen the soil, so I let them be.

My dad was no fool. He looked the other way when we stole his onions because my budding interest in his garden served a purpose. He soon had me weeding the rows of vegetables in his twenty-by-twenty-foot plot and generously allowed me to be the picker for dinner. He also allowed me to cut bouquets of his famous sweet peas for the table. Dad grew the best ones in the neighbourhood, on a chicken-wire screen that ran down one side of the vegetable garden. They never failed to lure me with their soft shades of pink, yellow, purple, and mauve, then to drown me in their scent.

My dad's vegetable patch, a 1940s Victory Garden grown to help the war effort as well as to satisfy his urge to garden, took

7

up more than a third of the sunniest part of the backyard, right behind the dining room. It was a marvel of geometric precision, and if I squinched my eyes its various shades and textures of green, accented with the rows of bright flowers Dad grew to attract bees, looked like the striped homespun draperies in our living room. The onions marched like succulent green soldiers in a tight row beside the sweet peas. Next grew a mounding row of bush beans; then feathery carrots; beets, their dark green leaves veined in red; curly kale; Brussels sprouts (which Bobbie, my younger sister, scorned as inedible, but which I adored for their slightly bitter crunch); frilly lime-green leaf lettuces; and yummy tomatoes made sweet by the long hours of prairie sun and staked with trimmings from Dad's woodworking projects. Zinnias and asters in pink, purple, and blue grew between a few of the rows, and the delicate stems and perky round leaves of shelling peas twined up a second wire screen at the other end of the patch, balancing the pattern perfectly. Under the dining room window a row of purple and yellow hollyhocks formed the fringed hem of my imagined draperies.

On summer holidays and weekends I spent most mornings in the vegetable patch, dabbling in the earth and pulling weeds until they imprinted themselves on the insides of my eyelids. "Pull from under the leaves, right where the stems come out of the ground," my dad would instruct me, folding his lanky frame beside me on the ground and tossing his hair back off his forehead in a familiar gesture. While I pulled I soaked up the music floating from the windows. Dad played operas and marches all day long on the record player, throwing in a few of Mom's favourite Beethoven sonatas to keep her happy. Her desires held sway when the World Series was on the radio in the fall, however; then *La Traviata* and "Colonel Bogey," gave way to the Cardinals and the New York Yankees.

Except for two giant lilac bushes and a dense growth of lily-of-the-valley behind the garage the rest of the yard was unremarkable, but the spot under the pine tree next to the vegetable garden was good for parental sitting. After dinner Dad would light a Sweet Cap in one of the two wide-armed wooden chairs he'd made, the kind called Adirondack or Muskoka chairs in home-design magazines today, and Mom would bring out her tea and knitting. Dad was inordinately proud of that pine tree, even though it was there when we moved into the house. It was a jack pine, he said, and rarely grew in the city. I was unimpressed by trees, but that pine must have had some presence because I can still picture its rough bark and feathery needles that whispered in the breeze. Back then I preferred the lilacs because, like the sweet peas, they had flowers that nearly bowled me over with their perfume. Dad also built the sturdy swing at the bottom of the garden. It was so tall it was the envy of the neighbourhood, but Mom was unsure of its safety. If Bobbie and I pumped hard enough, with her sitting on the flat wooden seat and me standing, legs astride her, we could rise so high that her feet would graze the top branches of the lilac and I could see over the board fence to the street beyond. This always sent Mom into near hysterics. "Stop it, stop it!" she'd shriek from the kitchen window. "You'll fall and be paralyzed forever!"

Ours was a busy house. We often had "company," as Mom called guests of any kind, even a neighbour over for morning coffee. "Company is coming," she'd sing out on summer Tuesdays when her book group was about to arrive and she was arranging her special rolled and layered sandwiches on platters. "Scoot outside now." Not that Bobbie and I cared to eavesdrop indoors on these more or less boring occasions. The Thursday supper club and the Saturday night couples bridge were different—then we hated being sent upstairs to our third-floor bedroom because we always knew from the drone of conversation followed by gales of laughter that we were missing something good. We learned on those evenings it was better to hang out with our grandparents, my father's parents, who had lived with us since I was six and Bobbie was two. They were Norman Rockwell sorts of grandparents, slightly padded in front and greying on top, indulgent of their only grandchildren; they loved to have us come up to their own special living room on the second floor, where they also had the biggest bedroom. While the jokes and laughter carried on below, Grandma crocheted edgings on bridge cloths or pillowcases and served us chocolate-chip cookies while Grandpa sang us silly little songs, incorporating our names into the lyrics wherever he could. As he sang he puffed on his pipe, filling and packing it from the thermidor Dad had made him for Christmas. We waited expectantly to see how our names would appear in "Frankie and Johnny" or "Abdul Abulbul Amir," giggling with delight when it happened. These evenings became almost as much fun as eavesdropping on our parents' parties, and even after Grandpa entered the veteran's hospital and then died there we continued to sit with Grandma on bridge and supper club nights.

I was named Elizabeth Ann in honour of my two grandmothers, but by the time I was two it seemed too big a name for a little girl, to say nothing of how hard it would have been to work into a song. It was Grandma who suggested I become Betty Ann instead, which turned out to be the first of a couple of name changes in my life. I always liked Bobbie's name better: she was christened Roberta because Dad fell for Irene Dunne in a 1935 movie with that title, and the name's short form suited her cute blondness to a T.

Our dad was something of an artisan, and he made many more lovely pieces in addition to tobacco thermidors for people at Christmas. Of course he had a real job, something to do with designing and selling new fluorescent lighting systems for offices, but his *real* work, at least as far as I could see, was in our basement. He'd come home from his job and head downstairs to his workroom, where he crafted pieces of choice mahogany and walnut into end tables, coffee tables, and fireside benches for our living room. Mom, ever the sewer and needlework artist, made gros point covers for the benches (she also made dresses and pyjamas and shorts for Bobbie and me). The basement also held a darkroom Dad had built for developing and printing the photographs he took on family outings and vacations. When the red bulb outside the door was lit we weren't allowed in, but at other times exploring it was fun. Bobbie and I loved watching the images magically appear on the thick, creamy paper Dad used for his prints, but we avoided the pans of vile-smelling liquid and the guillotine he used for trimming his pictures. While I was about twelve he gave up photography, however. "He figured he'd never be as good as Cartier-Bresson," my mother sighed, explaining to a grown-up me years later why he'd quit something he did so well and enjoyed so much. "Everything had to be an art piece." Well, maybe his pictures weren't the kind you'd hang in a gallery, but the play of light and shadow and the composition of his shots still look professional to me. And how wonderful it is today to have such a photographic record of our family and the places we visited.

For many years I didn't appreciate the skills my mom and dad exhibited, nor did I understand what harmony my family generally lived in. I wished for a more interesting family, like some of my friends. Two of them had older brothers who were off fighting the war and writing home about midnight missions over Germany or escorting troop ships across the Atlantic. One had a sister who was engaged to a U.S. Marine, probably the most romantic story I'd ever heard. Two friends had parents who had switched families—the mom of one had moved in with the dad of the other, and vice versa; we were too young to realize the full import of this, but we thought it was pretty silly, especially since they still were all friends together. Another friend had a father we'd sometimes find crawling in the bushes around their front porch when we went to her house after school, or digging in the earth like a child in a sandbox. Her mom always took us aside and asked us not to tell our parents about this, but of course I did. When I told Mom she looked alarmed, but I had no idea why. Was he a drunk or was he mentally ill? I guess I'll never know, but in either case his affliction wouldn't have been publicly acknowledged.

Our family's only distinguishing factor was my English grandma who, despite her patrician accent, perfectly waved grey hair, and modest pale pink lipstick, had an eccentric streak. Much to my mother's embarrassment, she flirted brazenly with deliverymen and was always sure to meet the postman at the front door in a close-fitting mauve sweater because he'd made the big mistake of admiring its colour one day. "I'm wearing your favourite sweater again!" she'd trill, her eyes batting as she took the mail from his hand. These antics didn't bother me, but her food habits did. She started her mornings with a glass of hot water and the juice of a lemon, followed by a glass of ice-cold water. "To clean out my system," she'd say to me. "It would be good for yours, too." Ugh. I couldn't stand the idea of her other diet alternatives, either: a pitcher of carrot juice a day, made in our new household blender; and wheat germ sprinkled over her evening meal, followed by a half dozen or so vitamin pills. Lately I've decided she was the original health food nut.

Our old three-storey frame house stood on a busy, tree-shaded street in Winnipeg, on a bus route and two blocks from the school my sister and I attended. Like all the houses on the street, it had a spacious front porch, and because our house was on a corner our porch wrapped around one side as well. The front section was screened in, making it a perfect place for play on mosquito-ridden summers when I was still young enough for a game of "house" with my sister. Actually, our game focused on cooking because a lot of that was done in our house and there were lots of "ingredients" in the garden and the local park to draw from. Nature was our larder, you might say. For plates we used the shiny round leaves of what I now know is bergenia but which Grandma called pig squeak because of the sound the thick leaves made when they were moved. Bergenia leaves doubled as frying pans for sautéing the poplar leaves picked from a neighbour's tree, which stood in for sliced potatoes; I especially liked these in the fall, when they turned pale yellow and really looked like Mom's fried potatoes. Our stove was an overturned cardboard shoebox with the elements drawn on in red crayon. The caragana hedge was a good provider: its slender green pods looked exactly like real green beans, but the tiny yellow flowers that came before the pods were especially valued because we could suck out the sweet nectar. They played themselves on our plates, a special dessert of our own invention. Unripe saskatoon berries were green peas; ripe ones went between two layers of leaves for a pie. Wild chamomile was valued for its fresh pineapple scent. Sometimes I'd sneak into the vegetable garden and pull a few immature, inch-long carrots for the real thing, and we'd tear up the leaves for spinach, which we hated in real life. Pine cones were Brussels sprouts; a feather from the wing of a bird was transformed into a chicken leg or a slice of roast beef. Feathers were only occasional finds, thank goodness, and we hoped they were lying there because the bird had put up a good fight escaping from the jaws of our ginger tom, Sandy. Twigs

23

broken into pieces represented the meat in a stew. Sometimes we even had a little laugh and sprinkled sand over our dinners in honour of Grandma's wheat germ.

It was lots of fun, and I think that examining the plants' parts closely to see what role they might play in my outdoor kitchen taught me a lot about how nature worked. Bobbie and I were usually left alone to exercise our imaginations for whole days without a parent or grandparent to interfere. No doubt part of the reason for non-intervention after I turned twelve was the debilitating stroke our dad suddenly suffered, which left him paralyzed on one side and unable to speak and which turned our household upside down. As kids, we didn't understand how serious this development was—although the bridge and supper clubs were gone we still had company who came to have tea and cookies and visit with our dad. Everybody liked our dad—he was a kindly man with a wry sense of humour he didn't seem to realize he had because he always looked vaguely surprised when someone laughed at one of his off-the-cuff comments. All this disappeared after he had his stroke and couldn't speak, and Bobbie and I missed his gentle teasing. After several months during which Mom helped him exercise his legs in bed, he started to practise walking again. When the frustration of trying so hard with so little success left him in tears, not at all a normal reaction for our supportive and independent father, Mom would usher Bobbie and me out of the living room and off to play.

Then I turned thirteen and outgrew my sister's companionship. My school friends, including some newly discovered boys, became much more interesting. My shape was changing and so did my name: my friends thought Betty Ann sounded like a character in a Pollyanna book, and I had to agree. I became Liz, a name I liked because it sounded sophisticated and a bit glamorous. In my new more grown-up role, bicycle rides out to the prairies replaced childish games of house and allowed me a wider exploration of nature.

The prairies outside Winnipeg were only about a mile from our house and were flat as far as the eye could see; sometimes I imagined climbing on a stepladder so that I could see over the horizon. My buddies and I would ride out on our bikes, knapsacks strapped to the handlebars, and set up little pup tents for the afternoon. We'd make a small fire and roast hot dogs. With my new name and my new-found freedom, I felt very grown up. We weren't far from home, but these trips were like going on safari, an adventure with no adults around to ask us to help with the dishes or tidy our rooms—just the leaves of trembling aspen fluttering silver and green in the hot breezes and stubby, short grasses hurting the soles of our feet if we walked barefoot. In the spring I'd admire sheets of pale mauve pasqueflower, which Dad called prairie crocus, and, later, its fluffy seed heads. In summer big bluestem undulated gracefully; purple prairie clover reminded me of Grandma's thimble with a frill of purple blossoms around its base; and the petals of pale purple coneflower drooped beautifully, like a ballerina in *Swan Lake*. Of course I didn't know the names of these plants back then, but I did know about *Swan Lake*, because Dad had taken me to see it.

The long, slow western dusks must have been enchanting on the prairie, too, but I had to savour them from the front steps or my bedroom window because I had to be off the prairie and home long before suppertime. I still miss the prairie dusks, when time seems to stand still for hours as the sky changes from vibrant pink and gold to mauve and deep purple before a grey haze obliterates all the colours of the landscape except the whites. A different painting every night; a masterpiece if there are clouds to reflect a rainbow of colours.

But my youthful reverie didn't last, and I got my wish to be part of a family that people found compelling enough to talk about. When I was fourteen our dad suddenly suffered another stroke from which he never regained consciousness. This tragic event changed the direction of our lives. As they say, sometimes it's better not to get what you wish for.

CHAPTER 2

The

JOURNEY BEGINS

. . . . .

ALL MY FRIENDS except for the boys came to my father's funeral. Seeing them there lining the sidewalk and looking so solemn and sorry for me when Mom, Bobbie, and I followed the coffin down the funeral home steps made me fall into a heap of tears. It wasn't really the kind of stardom among my peers that I'd been looking for.

Two weeks later I had to say goodbye to my pals when we left Winnipeg to move in with Mom's family in southern Ontario. You might think this was an incredibly short time for Mom to make such a major change in our lives, but the move had been planned for months. It was clear after a year of therapy that Dad would never be able to hold a regular job or do his beloved carpentry work again, and we would have to scale down our lives. Until Dad regained more strength and he and Mom somehow put their lives back together, we would live with Granny on the farm Mom had grown up on, just outside the little village of Paisley in Ontario's Bruce County. We had to leave Grandma, too; she decided it would be awkward for her to join us, and she made plans to move out west to live with some cousins.

I have another vivid film clip in my mind of the scene of our departure, leaving our home to go to our new life. It's a glorious Winnipeg day, and we are climbing into our neighbour's car for the trip to the railway station. I have on my brand new fawn dress, the one I wore to Dad's funeral; Mom is wearing her flowered print dress, a hat and gloves, and her everything-is-all-right face. Bobbie is in her best outfit, a pleated navy jumper and frilly blouse, her hair in neat ringlets. Bobbie and I are quiet; Mom is trying to make conversation with her dear friends, and she doesn't look back. I do: right through the open gate into the backyard. The two wooden chairs still sit under the pine tree, now the property of the new owners. The Victory Garden is in ruins, as it had been the previous summer. Sandy grooms himself in a pool of sunshine, unaware that he will never see us again. "He's too old; he'll never survive with all those wild barn cats," Mom had said. I long to run to him for one last cuddle. The scene ends at this point, with my throat closing up.

And here is something I regret to this day: I never told my mom or my dad how excited I actually was to be breaking new ground, so to speak, to be starting fresh in another community. My poor dad felt guilty about taking Bobbie and me away from our Winnipeg friends and our more advantaged urban schools, especially me, on the brink of adulthood. Even though he could barely make himself understood, he tried to explain why our lives were about to change, and how sorry he was, because it was his fault. Tears would come to Mom's eyes when she took me aside later to tell me what he was trying to say. I, the typical selfish adolescent, decided to hold this trump card close to my chest in case I needed it later. Or did I think of it that callously? Perhaps I just preferred being the centre of attention for a while in a house where life-and-death drama was being played out every day, where the needs of a man I'd looked up to as a protector and teacher suddenly were far more important than my adolescent angst.

Travelling by train to Granny's house, something we'd done many summers of our lives, was my childhood's introduction to the geographic diversity of this country, as well as my first experience with luxury dining—white linen tablecloths in the dining car, smoked Lake Winnipeg goldeye followed by finger bowls with a thin slice of lemon floating on perfectly lukewarm water. I thought it was soup on our first trip and spooned it to my mouth, to the delight of the smiling black man serving us. I'd never seen a black person before, and I was as fascinated by him as he was amused by me.

Two nights and a day or two days and a night was the choice of schedules to Toronto that the railway offered, and Dad always insisted we board at night because he was convinced Bobbie and I would never sit still for two full days on a train. So we left the flat, golden prairies in the evening, were rocked to sleep by the hypnotic *clickety-clack, clickety-clack* of the wheels on the track, and awakened to the rugged trees and vast, rocky wilderness of northern Ontario. Travelling by train was like moving along in a comfortable cocoon where time passed on one level as we ate, slept, and observed our fellow travellers while the country rushed past at top speed: pine trees, rocks, rivers. Then we'd stop at a junction point and step out of the train to meet stillness; we'd stretch our legs and smell the wondrous air, scented with wood and pine sap and smoke, not to mention the diesel fuel of the train.

The next morning I could hardly wait to raise the blind and see the changing terrain: some rocks, yes, lots of lakes and evergreens rising in points, but many small towns and railway crossings; then rolling countryside with orchards filled with apple trees, the pretty fields edged with split-rail fences or piles of stones dragged there long ago by farmers as they cleared the land—glacial till, Dad had told me, broken pieces of ancient rocks left there by glaciers as they were melting millennia ago.

As the train raced towards Toronto the landscape gradually became more urban, but there was always some landscape to look at, to admire. Years later I read a quote that made me think of my train-window experiences. In *The History of the Modern Taste in Gardening*, Horace Walpole, the eighteenth-century British writer (and the fourth Earl of Oxford), said rather grandly of landscape designer William Kent, one of the originators of the Landscape Movement, that "he leaped the fence and saw all nature was a garden." The Landscape Movement espoused the idea that all gardens of any consequence should copy nature, and I wondered why this notion hadn't occurred to someone before the eighteenth century. All a nature-loving traveller, even a very young one, has to do is look out a train window and see that the landscape is its own garden, and Mother Nature perhaps the best designer. The unwitting irony in Walpole's statement is that Kent and his cohort, Capability Brown, actually had little empathy for real landscapes; theirs were idealized to the extreme, and the pair had no compunction about removing trees or rerouting streams, even moving whole villages, if they didn't fit into one of their "natural" designs.

As we neared Granny's farm, having transferred in Toronto to a now long-retired steam train, my eyes remained glued to the passing gardens. To this day they are as lovely to my eye as any that Kent or Brown might have designed: rolling hills and streams, copses of trees, the roadsides and ditches graced with the giant single stalks of yellow flowers on velvety-leaved mullein, standing like architectural exclamation points, or with clumps of dainty white ox-eye daisies bobbing in the breeze, and the finely cut foliage and filmy flowers of Queen Anne's lace. Bright low buttercups and foxtail grass that reminded me of brand new artist's paintbrushes rushed past the window near the train bed, and the flat green rosettes of plantain. It was named white-man's foot by the Ojibway because wherever the white man walked plantain followed him, till it spread over all of North America. Like many other flowers that have become naturalized here, the ox-eye daisy and Queen Anne's lace were brought to North America by settlers to remind them of the gardens of home, but plantain was valued more for the medicinal value of its leaves and seeds.

In the structured gardens around the yellow or red brick farm and village houses grew vining purple clematis, hollyhocks and delphiniums, silver dollar plants, orange day lilies and hostas. Hostas were called plantain lilies then, and I considered them utterly boring because they were too *green*: their leaves dominated, and the thin stalks of small white flowers seemed so insignificant they disappeared. I grow them enthusiastically today, having had a change of heart now that they've been considerably hybridized. Today hostas are *de rigueur* in every garden, and they come in hundreds of varieties with leaves quilted or smooth, pointed or round, in chartreuse or blue-green or countless patterns of green, cream, and white; the flowers have been improved as well and grow in showy stalks of purple, mauve, and white. Too often the new varieties that come on the market are so much like the ones introduced the previous year that you can't tell them apart, making me wonder if things haven't gone a little too far in the hybridization department.

Although Mom had grown up in Paisley she'd been away a long time, so we were exotic new inhabitants. Every Saturday night after we finished the chores we'd leave the farm and drive with Granny and Uncle Ren into town, a mile distant, to shop for groceries and socialize on the streets outside the stores, as people liked to do in this village of seven hundred. I'd often catch some of the women casting pitying glances towards my sister and me, the two skinny little fatherless girls. I rather basked in the limelight of being a half-orphan.

My mom, my young and pretty mom who bore her grief like the stoic she was, was enfolded and supported by her family, but I don't remember her talking much during that period. I do remember quiet weeping in the dark of night, when Bobbie, next to me in the big brass bed, would poke me and say, "Mommy is sad again."

My own loss I really didn't understand. Except for the shock of finding my father unconscious on the day he died, twitching and snorting horribly in the hospital bed that had been set up in our dining room, and the terrible finality of seeing the coffin lid close over his face in the funeral home—an untimely move by the mortician, I'm sure—I was curiously detached. Years would pass before I realized what I was missing. As for Bobbie, just turned ten, she hardly seemed affected at all, but she confided to me years later that she couldn't remember a thing of her life previous to our dad's death except for the stories Mom and I told her.

Life was good with my new expanded family. Granny's farm was adjacent to two farms belonging to aunts and uncles, one beside hers and the other across the highway leading into Paisley. On Granny's farm I explored the wonders of the pasture (carefully avoiding the cow-pies), the ancient apple trees in the orchard (which offered all kinds of climbing possibilities), the henhouse with its magic cache of eggs, and the grasses and the wildflowers that grew with abandon over the fields, which my cousins, my sister, and I would walk through at dusk on the

way from one homestead to the other after a family supper. I felt
at home in the fields, as if the grasses and the wildflowers and
weeds knew me and welcomed me to spend some time with them.
The sweet smell of the grass filled me with a longing I still feel
to this day when I drive in the country with the windows open.

I even liked the smell of the manure pile behind my uncle's
barn. It had a hidden sweetness beneath the stink of decay and,
like the strong scent of the skunks that made their presence
known in the night, it had a visceral appeal for my adolescent
nose. My Uncle Ren used to tease me about it. "Give her a whiff
of eau de manure and she'll get happy!" he'd say when I was in
a teenage funk. Years later, when I had a house and family and
garden of my own in the city and came up on weekend visits,
Uncle Ren, who had become my gardening mentor, although
neither one of us had heard the word at the time, would load
up bushel baskets of the stuff—well rotted and unsmelly in its
maturity, I assure you—and I'd take it home in the trunk of the
car. My kids had to make room for the suitcases in the back seat.

Our cousins were built-in playmates, and we spent afternoons picking wildflowers and raspberries along the railroad
tracks or making up games to play in the fields and the barns:
contests to see who could be the first to find ten fresh cow-pies
(extra points for one that was still warm); games of potentially
dangerous hide-and-seek among the pitchforks and old scythes
in the barn and hayloft, which Mom put a stop to the day she
found one of us hiding our eyes against a cow stall while counting to one hundred. My favourite was our acted-out episodes of
Flash Gordon, space explorer, using the rusted '39 Ford in the
field behind the barn as the spaceship. I, of course, insisted on
playing Dale Arden, Flash's beautiful sidekick. They were such
innocent games compared with the urban-chase computer games
of today; how ancient—and blessed—they make me feel!

23

Evenings were devoted to both outdoor and indoor pursuits: watching the fireflies in the orchard or lying in the pasture and counting falling stars, or playing in family sessions of poker or crokinole by the light of my aunt's new Aladdin kerosene lamps (our farms, even though they were only a short distance from the village, still had no electricity). We played poker with buttons kept for the purpose, around a dining room table that could be expanded to hold a dozen or more hired men when threshing season rolled around.

Our uncles teased us mercilessly. They'd poke fun at my long, lank hair, which I fancied was a darker version of Lana Turner's. On dark and moonless nights they'd scare us by cloaking themselves in white sheets and the big plaid car rug, holding on their heads the dusty stuffed owls Granny kept on the landing of the staircase. *Tap tap tap* . . . the owls' beaks on the kitchen window would get our attention. *WOOooo . . . woooo . . . wooo . . .* the uncles would wail. We, of course, were hardly fooled, but we shivered deliciously and screamed nonetheless. Now I realize that in our restrained household, teasing and humour took the place of hugs, kisses, and tears and helped us along our road of bereavement.

Uncle Ren was the principal uncle. He lived at Granny's part-time because he was the high-school principal in a neighbouring town; he was also the organist at one of our village churches and a serious gardener. He helped my mom in her need, but he also helped me with algebra and geometry, although I'm sure my stubbornness frustrated him. But we discovered that we shared a love of nature and of growing things. I trotted behind him in his garden in front of Granny's house, holding transplants and weeding when called on, although I must confess Uncle Ren wasn't as much for weeding as my father had been. Ren believed in dense planting that hid the little monsters, and sometimes he just ignored them. He consistently beat the ladies of the community at the fall fair, winning ribbons for his roses, his carefully nurtured dinner-plate-size dahlias, and his single spikes of lush, cobalt-blue delphiniums displayed in preserving jars, and for his wild strawberry jelly. My sister and my cousins and I were happy to spread it on our toast, but we really didn't appreciate how much work went into picking the tiny berries that grew along the railroad tracks in front of the farm and how small the yield was from a big bucket of berries after the seeds had been strained out in Granny's cloth jelly bag.

Uncle Ren's gardens were much admired in our community. Beside the expected farm vegetable garden his flower border grew wider and wider as he bought or raised more plants. It was an English-style border filled with big clumps of plants—the prize-winning roses, delphiniums, and immense dahlias, plus purple, mauve, and pink Canterbury bells, crisp, white shasta daisies with yellow centres, purple and yellow irises, and on and on. And he had something I'd never seen—a greenhouse. His was a small homemade plastic one, leaning against the side of the shed, and in it he raised new cultivars of old-fashioned favourites from seed, started tomatoes for planting out in late May, and wintered over exotic bulbs he bought from a Toronto supplier.

Uncle Ren was a born gardener who didn't stop till the day he died. Years later, after he'd retired and I was an experienced gardener, he keeled over one Sunday morning while playing the organ at church—with his boots on, my sister and I joked, in a reverent kind of way. If it had happened a few hours later, he would have literally succumbed with his wellies on and a spade in his hand.

The funny thing is, if you can think of it as funny, dying with your boots on seems to be a bit of a family tradition. A few

25

years before Ren met his maker, Mom died the same way. She'd lived a long, full life during which she never seemed to sit down, and one day when she was shopping with Uncle Ren in a big new mall in a nearby town, she felt terribly tired. Ren took her to the hospital and, with her packages still in his car, she slipped away, taking her last breath peacefully and with acceptance, without the strength to leave a last word for Bobbie and me, who couldn't get to the hospital from Toronto in time. A decade later Bobbie also died unexpectedly and shockingly—and, like our Dad, far too young—on a plane on her way to a business seminar in Texas. Mom and Bobbie both died in winter, leaving me to feel even more alone without my garden to help console me.

A FEW MILES south of Paisley lay the Greenock Swamp, a spooky, scary-sounding place. "Just one big dark forest, like a giant sponge," Uncle Ren, ever the teacher seizing the opportunity to impart knowledge, would say to us. "It soaks up water when it rains. . . *thluuurp*. . . and blows it out when things are dry." I imagined it as a giant mouth sucking up bad kids in one big gulp and spewing them out later in little pieces.

One of my aunts contributed her own swamp stories, about how in the nineteenth century, long before her time, canals and a railway carried white pine out of its dense interior to make ship masts for the Royal Navy. The rail lines kept sinking, and after twenty-five years the company finally gave up, having harvested five million board feet of pine every year. But I liked best the story about certain great uncles of ours from another town. "Back in Prohibition," my aunt would intone as she waited for the kettle to boil on the woodstove, pausing dramatically, ". . . back in Prohibition they made moonshine down there in the deepest parts of the swamp. We heard they smuggled it across the lake to Detroit and made a fortune. But they were never caught."

I was afraid of the swamp and found no reason to venture anywhere near it, but I did explore the fields as far away as we were allowed to go. That was relatively far, since our three family farms were so close to each other and we had Buck, my uncles' border collie, to protect us. Buck had lost a leg in an encounter with some farm machinery, but the accident hadn't affected his intelligence. He was the smartest animal I'd ever met. "Go get the cows," an uncle would whisper in his cocked ear after supper, and Buck, ears flattened and moving like a bullet on three legs through the fields, body low and circling, would have those placid, slow-moving bovines in the barn in ten minutes.

Buck knew the countryside like the back of his paw. On hot days he'd lead me back to the shade of the woodlot, where the pure white starry flowers of bloodroot and the tri-petalled white trilliums poked through last year's dead leaves in spring; in summer lacy ferns abounded, plus the tall, arching, and alternating leaves of false Solomon's seal, which made me hunt for the small white flowers hidden underneath. *So much white and green in here!* I'd think to myself, not knowing the names of the woodland plants and glad for the brighter colours of Ren's garden. Buck didn't linger in the woodlot—his destination was the shallow golden-watered river behind my aunt's farm across the highway. There he'd splash happily and I'd wade gingerly, leery of the bloodsuckers that attached themselves to Bobbie and me one day, prompting us to run screaming back to my aunt's farmhouse, where she poured lashings of salt on the slimy creatures until they loosened their hold and fell into the grass.

These were all new experiences to be learned from. I'd never encountered swamps or deep woodlots or yellow rivers harbouring bloodsuckers on the prairies. Even the shape of the land was different. Our new neck of the woods was, and still is, grain country—alfalfa, barley, and corn in sweeps of green and tawny tan, according to the season and the year; joyful, fruitful rolling fields that make you want to sing. It's cattle country, too, and I confess I had rather exaggerated this point to my friends in Winnipeg, boasting about my uncles' "ranches" where they raised cattle and sheep for the market, when in fact they were making modest livings as farmers just as their parents, including my grandfather, had done before them. I also quickly learned that although the Ontario sunsets were beautiful, they couldn't begin to compare with the long prairie dusks I'd known. Still, they were achingly lovely to me, and filled me with a longing for something I couldn't put my finger on, but I'm sure it had something to do with green-onion sandwiches. I'd sit on the steps of Granny's porch and drink in great pools of soft, perfumed air. I'd listen to my world settle down for the night, and I'd wonder who I was and where life would take me.

The future seemed a long way off, but the road was changing. I was growing up. Before school started a year later, we moved off the farm and into Paisley so that Bobbie and I could get to school more easily, and I fell into puppy love with the United Church minister's son and became best friends with the Baptist minister's daughter. These were two of seven churches in town, a not-unusual ratio for the villages in the area of about one for every hundred souls. But in our relentlessly Protestant and essentially dour Scots village, none was Catholic. Few people had even met a Catholic; when I later brought up my Catholic boyfriend and future husband from the city he was viewed by some of the older folk as if he were the devil himself.

In town I learned to cook, too. Mom had charged me with making dinners while she was working—she'd got a job at the local butcher shop—and I decided I loved cooking almost as much as helping Ren in the garden and exploring the countryside. I experimented with exotica like chile con carne and stuffed beef heart, which Mom ate dutifully, exclaiming over its nice oniony stuffing, and which made Bobbie gag—me too, to be honest. Mom bought me a cookbook, and I made stews and roasted pork chops and baked cookies and wanted to try everything on its pages. When I took a plate of Parker House rolls to the butcher shop to be admired and tasted, the owner exclaimed that I would make some man a fine wife one day. These were the days before feminism, and I was fifteen years old, so I took his remark as a compliment.

Uncle Ren had a new pursuit, too—a wide flower border behind our little rented house in town. His gardening experiments became more ambitious: over the next couple of years he grafted ten varieties of apples on the apple tree beside the porch—an amazing feat I would never have thought possible. I was suitably impressed, and by the next spring he had a serious helper: I couldn't cook all the time, and the fields were no longer near enough to easily explore, so I transferred my botanical interests wholly to his garden.

I'm not certain he wanted my help, because I think that for Ren, just as it is for me now, gardening was a solitary pursuit with its own rewards, and that didn't include naïve nieces. But I kept quiet and he put up with me, and gradually we developed a gardeners' bond. "Look at the buds on that delphinium!" he'd exclaim. "That's going to be a beauty." And we'd both marvel at the number of fat babies developing along the stem and nod at each other in silent understanding that they could mean a fall fair medal—his, of course, not mine.

The border behind our house kept growing as he divided plants in the farm garden and paid visits to nurseries in the city. I rather disapproved of its sometimes unkempt look, having spent a few years watching my dad as he planted vegetables in careful rows and edged and weeded assiduously. But I said nothing

29

for fear that I would be asked to dig out the grass in the heavy clay soil and instead pulled out weeds after a softening rain or clipped off spent flowers with Mom's nail scissors. And this was an English flower border, after all, where plants shouldn't be placed in military rows! Even I knew that, having perused Ren's gardening books.

Ren was practising Edwardian cottage-style gardening, although I'm sure he, like me, had never heard of it. He was just following fashion, one that was started in the 1870s by William Robinson and taken up by Gertrude Jekyll, a garden designer who romanticized the notion of the humble worker's garden and raised it to high style, designing the gardens of rich people with drifts of plants that bloomed in waves of colour and tumbled over fences and onto gravel pathways. Today when I look out my kitchen window I see echoes of Uncle Ren's garden in my own. I'm more careful about weeds than Ren was, maybe because sometimes people come to tour my garden and I have to keep up my reputation. I've also learned a thing or two: if you don't have much grass you don't need to do much edging. But I've never had any luck growing delphiniums, and prize roses elude me.

Within a few short years Dad's fears that the move to such a small village might affect Bobbie and me proved to be well founded, at least as far as I was concerned. I soon lost interest in Uncle Ren's garden and the basic three Rs that our small school taught, and I yearned for more adventurous pursuits. With the confidence of youth I thought the time had come for me to seek fame and fortune in the city. I had decided I was meant to be a fashion model, for I had inherited my father's thin, leggy bone structure and my mother's photogenic face, and that career wouldn't require a university degree.

My decision prompted no arguments and no tears that I was aware of. Mom couldn't afford higher education for my sister and me, and there were no opportunities in our small community beyond clerking in a grocery store or working in the bank. I was sixteen, and I lacked a high-school diploma. Once I had teenagers of my own I wondered how Mom had ever let me go at such a tender age, but she agreed that it was time for me to find my own way, my own life. For me, it was an adventure.

So off to Toronto I went, my hopes high, feeling that I was stepping out into the real world, at last.

CHAPTER 3

☖

My

FIRST GARDEN

. . . . .

Toronto was riding the crest of the postwar wave when I
arrived in 1948. Jobs were plentiful, a suburban housing
boom was underway, and the university was overflowing
with returned servicemen taking advantage of the government's
offer of a free education. At least a dozen of them were living in
the family-run boarding house that was my new home.

I was a teenager with an impossible dream. How green I
was! I had little education, a brand new but menial job as a filing
assistant in a food products manufacturing company, Stafford
Industries Ltd. (obtained through the good graces of its owner,
a success story from our village), and paid-up tuition for a
course at a modelling school. One day soon, I was sure, I would
be walking fashion-show runways in New York or be featured
on the cover of *Vogue*. If only I'd had a crystal ball to see how
different life would be. Gardening was already in my blood,
even if I didn't realize it, and my real talents—I didn't have the
chutzpa or the grace to be a model—were germinating quietly
beneath my dreams.

Twenty-one tenants, all of them older than me by at least five years, plus the landlady's family of five and a cook, shared the spacious boarding house, formerly an elegant private residence on Bernard Avenue, in what's now called the East Annex. I felt as though I was living in the bosom of a new family, and some of its members have remained in my life in one way or another to this day. It was hard for all of us not to appreciate the handsome architecture of the house we shared or its fine interior appointments: an original stained-glass window on the landing of the wide oak stairway; a panelled, banquet-size dining room with a fireplace (perfect for the boarding-house table); bathrooms as big as my present bedroom, with tubs six feet long; a small panelled library with a fireplace nook and built-in seating. The library opened onto a large concrete porch, which in turn stepped down into a rose garden.

The other boarders, too busy with their studies or their art assignments (for there were many art students living there, too), seldom went into the garden, so I could admire it alone and spin tales about it in my head. It was indeed a secret garden, walled and overgrown and untended like the one in Frances Hodgson Burnett's book, but subtly revealing the beauty of its structure under the branches and weeds. My imaginary inhabitants were older than the children in Burnett's book, more on the order of Jane Austen characters. I saw hoop-skirted young ladies, the daughters of the house, strolling the stone paths of its four-square design between the rose and herb beds, pausing to read the time in the centre sundial. They were awaiting the arrival of young lovers. Through the lovely arched gate the young swains finally came; they bowed and delicately raised ivory hands to gentle lips, then separated to sit as couples on the stone benches surrounding the garden...

The house existed in the eighteenth century only in my romantic imagination. It was designed in 1906 by a well-known architect, Eden Smith, and was an upper-class home until it was transformed into our boarding house. It underwent several more changes after the landlady sold it and the boarders had gone on to other lives, from rooming house to self-contained bachelor suites, with those lovely spacious bedrooms turned into small flats with stoves and cupboards and toilets installed in one corner. Happily, the house was eventually returned to its former glory as a private residence, and in the '90s it was designated as a historical residence by a Toronto bylaw. It entered my life again a few years later in a most unexpected way, but that story comes later.

The city thrilled me. It held such promise, such sophistication, even though in retrospect I realize it was almost as dour and impossibly conservative as the village I'd come from, not at all like the hub of many cultures and customs it's become. It was autumn, and the leaves on the thousands of trees in the city were turning gold and red and yellow and giving off a sweet yet faintly acidic scent, just like the ones that grew in Paisley. On Sundays, when everything but the churches were closed, my roommate and I would walk for miles, exploring the streets downtown and north to Casa Loma, then hopping the streetcar to walk through the wildness of High Park. This city was almost as exciting as I knew New York would be.

Of course, I never made it to New York. Fate intervened in the form of a handsome young man with Tony Curtis hair and hazel eyes. One day he entered the filing room from the sales office of the food products company, and it was love at first sight. His name was Joe—I had never known a boy with that name before, and it somehow made him seem more exotic.

Being children of our time, once things got serious we got married. There was nothing else to do—fooling around in the car was okay, but if you wanted more you made it official. That was just the way things were, and I was too scared to challenge convention and risk pregnancy even if some of my friends did. We were far too young to get married, of course—I was still in my teens—and there were warning signs, even if I didn't recognize them at the time. Joe was a bit of a "lone wolf," confided his mother, who had taken me to her heart, and she was glad he was going out with me because it might make him more sociable. Then Joe told me he didn't like my name. "Liz is too *sharp* for you," he said, "Let's call you something else." I thought changing my identity might be fun, but realized years later Joe's remark was one of the signs I should have heeded. And so I became Robin to everyone I met for the next twenty years, returning to Liz only after I'd decided to leave the marriage.

But our early days were happy enough, and life seemed to be unfolding as it should: the thought of a career in modelling had vanished, and I had graduated from my menial filing job to a more glamorous one as a personal shopper at Simpsons, a large downtown department store. We were young marrieds ready to adopt the traditional lifestyle of our parents, with a new apartment and new furniture, and company for dinner often enough that I could practise my cooking skills.

My only garden was a windowsill, where I valiantly tried to grow the African violets my mother-in-law kept pressing on me, along with the proper containers to hold them and detailed instructions on their cultivation, which I dutifully followed. She gave me a long tray filled with pebbles so that I could water them from below—even a few droplets of water would damage their fleshy leaves and cause a fungus to set in, she warned— and several pots of the little monsters to set on it. I had purple ones, pink ones, singles, miniatures, and one of her very special doubles. They sat on moistened gravel in the tray in a window facing east, in as much strong but indirect light as I could

35

provide. I fertilized carefully, not too much but not too little, as she instructed. I gave the pots a quarter turn every other day so that they'd get even light, and I clipped off the dying leaves and flowers.

I'm not of the school that believes plants have souls, or even feelings, and talking to them has always suggested an unstable mind to me, but I wonder if these little beauties knew down in their earthy little hearts that I detested them. They inevitably withered and died. Maybe they died for spite. My mother-in-law was always a little disappointed about their demise, but she persevered, being an accepting person supportive of this child-woman who had become her daughter-in-law.

She had a lovely backyard garden, too, with raised beds around the periphery of my in-laws' small lot filled with carefully tended perennials and annuals, and a rose of Sharon tree with big pink hibiscuslike blooms in late summer, of which she was justifiably proud. I always complimented her garden, and she was happy that someone in the family actually appreciated her efforts, although I secretly thought her borders couldn't compare with Uncle Ren's. They looked a little stiff to me, and too narrow. Looking back I realize I had already internalized Ren's love of wild, untamed cottage-style gardens, with plants sensuously falling over each other in their haste to show themselves off. I also came to realize a few years later that callow youth are unbearably narrow-minded in their judgment of what is pleasing or worthwhile and what is not. I often wish I'd been able to demonstrate my eventual maturity and insights to my mother-in-law, but after I left her son many years later she refused to speak to me. She forgave me at the end of her life, but by then it was too late for personal revelations.

My mother-in-law and her garden were godsends after the first baby came along and I began to feel jittery and anxious.

She said I had "baby blues" and my unease would go away in a few weeks once my hormones settled down and the baby got past the colicky stage. But I was more than blue—at times I felt breathless and anxious, as though I were looking down on the world from another plane. Sometimes I was downright agitated. My mother-in-law's doctor said I wasn't physically ill—I just needed to adjust to life. But what was wrong with me? I had a darling new baby boy, named Joe after his father and paternal grandfather, a good family to support me, a husband who didn't know how to deal with my strange feelings but seemed willing to wait things out. My mother-in-law came to my rescue many times by fetching me on summer afternoons, and I'd sit on a deck chair with tea near one of her borders while she happily cooed over the baby. I might even weed a little before we dined on one of her delicious suppers, with the dishes later whisked away before I could even offer to help. Those days gave me my first taste of the curative effects of a long sit and a bit of puttering in a pleasant garden, and gradually my symptoms subsided.

After the arrival a couple of years later of our second boy, a perfectly behaved baby we named Matthew, we bought a bungalow in the suburbs. It was shiny new, with satiny hardwood floors (of course we could hardly wait till we could afford to cover them with broadloom; polished floors were for our parents' generation), and an expanse of new sod in the front. The back was bare earth—not even good earth, as it turned out, just sandy subsoil with all the good stuff removed from the top—and it was our responsibility to add grass and a garden. I viewed it as an empty slate, where there would be a garden, a swing set and sandbox, and a place to barbecue.

It was the '50s, and the front lawn was king. All down our street the green carpet rolled out, interrupted only by asphalt driveways (a perk provided by the developer of our subdivision, as was the front sod) and edged on the house side by carbon-copy evergreen foundation plantings. A couple of varieties of junipers were the local favourite: most people planted several spreading, arching Pfitzer varieties too close to the picture windows, and columnar Skyrocket junipers at the house corners and sometimes each side of the entrance, too. I accepted all of these features as the natural thing to do. There was also an unwritten rule that every front lawn should be centred with a tree, and we were fortunate enough not to have to plant an immature sapling—we had a mature apple tree, a refugee of the orchard that once occupied the land our subdivision was built on. It was a McIntosh, with fragrant pink-white blossoms in spring and edible fruit in fall, as long as we pruned and sprayed as we should. It reminded me of the apple trees in Granny's orchard.

I left the front yard mostly to Joe, who bought the requisite power mower, a new oscillating sprinkler, bags of fertilizer, and cans of pesticides and herbicides, and I turned my attention to the back. Within weeks we had the lushest front lawn on the street but little in the back to crow over. When it was my turn to start a garden from scratch, despite my admiration for Ren's borders and my near disdain for my mother-in-law's tended beds, I didn't know where to begin.

Making a new garden is a challenge even for experienced gardeners. To one as green as me it was a mountain to climb. I suppose novice painters or sculptors feel the same combination of promise and uncertainty when faced with a blank canvas or a hunk of stone. I've learned since, simply through the experience of making several gardens and by reading the advice of experts, that the first step is to live with the space for a full year to see how you naturally make use of it, to become familiar with where the sun and shade fall, where the snow stays till late April and where it melts in March. Only then will you be familiar enough with your space to know how to fill it with a garden that both thrives and fulfills your needs.

But even if I'd known that then I didn't have the time to ruminate over purpose or design—the wind was quickly carrying the light, sandy soil from the backyard into the house through the open windows and leaving a film on every surface. So we laid sod to hold down the dirt and then we put in a hedge—Siberian elm, of all plants (sometimes mistakenly called Chinese elm, a slightly more desirable variety), because someone told us it would grow quickly and hide the ugly chain-link fence along the back of the property. Siberian elm has small leathery leaves that create a dense background, but it's really a tree and a very fast-growing one at that; that's why people often grow it as a hedge. When you're young, you want instant gratification, but years later, after I'd moved out, that unpruned hedge had grown into over-reaching trees that obliterated whatever garden was left. As far as I'm concerned Siberian elm is a thug.

It was midsummer before I started to think seriously about the back garden, a little late for starting one, and I was feeling anxious and jittery again. A garden wasn't high on my priority list; my emotional state was a higher concern. Many times I was sweating and panicky for no apparent reason, my heart beating so fast I thought I would die. My "baby blues" had turned into something more ominous, and even though I felt fine much of the time, at others I often couldn't get past the end of the driveway even while holding on to the baby carriage without dizziness, palpitations, and a feeling of impending doom. I was afraid that if my panic got out of control I was going to cause myself or my babies some harm or that I was going to go wild, screaming crazy some morning after my husband left for work.

I hid these feelings as much as I could, hardly speaking of my inner turmoil. I knew my mom and my mother-in-law felt worried but impotent, and there were murmurs of "nervous breakdown" when my mom visited and they talked, thinking I was out of earshot. I was certain Joe thought I was already crazy. Once he snapped at me that I had become a clinging vine, an accusation that shocked me. I knew I wasn't by nature dependent. I'd loved to scour unfamiliar fields with only Buck as my companion when I was a kid, and I'd enthusiastically come to Toronto on my own at a tender age, but something had changed me. At heart all I really wanted was to feel like my old self, to be free of the conflicts and anxiety that had overtaken me. I dealt with my panic attacks by trying to avoid them, an approach that meant never going to the movies or a restaurant, or even to a neighbour's for coffee, if panic threatened. I also limited my trips to the supermarket, a rather necessary job for a young mother with a family to prepare meals for; a couple of times I fled leaving a nearly full shopping cart behind me.

The garden—or rather my future garden—became my refuge. In much the same way as I'd found some kind of connection with the landscape as I roamed the fields with Buck on the farm, I found comfort in my own modest outdoor space. That first year, even though it was midsummer, I planted gorgeous large-flowered tuberous begonias in a large planter built onto the front of the house. They were prizewinners, raised and wintered over for years by Uncle Ren, and I was lucky to have them. First I filled the planter with bags and bags of soil bought at a nursery, loving the feel of it as it fell through my fingers into the planter and inhaling the smell of Mother Earth, then I nestled in the budding tubers, which soon delivered a punch of huge rose- and salmon-coloured flowers. Then we planted a weeping mulberry near the dining room window, next to where little Matthew slept out in his carriage. I thought that when the tree bore fruit later in the summer I'd make jam, but the birds got there first. One morning I woke up to a great chirping and commotion; the tree was alive and the fruit was gone in what seemed like seconds. Ever after that we left the fruit for the birds; they loved it so much.

The next spring I started my back garden. I'd noticed that when the neighbourhood toddlers came to play with mine, they gravitated towards the shade of a large tree in one of the rear corners. Aha!. . . the perfect place for their swing and sandbox. (Even if I didn't know it then, I was already learning something.) Along the back of the house, which had a southern exposure and warm brick, I decided to plant my favourite tomatoes. As for the rest, flower borders down each side would have to suffice—imagination failed me.

First I started the tomato bed—a wide one that would hold many plants. Who can live without fresh, homegrown tomatoes? I'd eaten them from my dad's garden and from Uncle Ren's, and they were a priority. As soon as the kids went down for their naps, I'd go out with my spade and fork, removing sod and shaking it out, putting the soil back in the bed and throwing the grass roots in the corner of the yard to rot as they chose. It was hot work because it always took place in the middle of the day, in a spot where the sun glanced off the brick and created an oven. I dug in some new soil and my uncle's well-rotted horse manure, and I planted beefsteak tomato seedlings Ren had raised in his little plastic greenhouse. Almost every day I worked till sweat was running off the end of my nose and I was ready to drop, but the effort and the smell of the earth helped calm my overactive psyche, and the sweat I felt was honest sweat, not the feeling that my bones and flesh were turning to water.

No one told me gardening was therapeutic; therapy wasn't a fashionable idea in those days and to admit to needing it would have been shameful. Today the idea of gardening as therapy has almost become a cliché—all gardeners I know mention it as a valuable side effect of their avocation, and courses in horticultural therapy, where you learn how to help alcoholics or the clinically depressed by introducing them to horticulture, are readily available. But gardens have provided safety and succour to humans for centuries. It's not hard for me to picture the neolithic gardener gradually beginning to derive pleasure and relaxation from her plot and to look for ways to make the plantings beautiful as well as useful.

Indeed, we know from tomb paintings and reliefs that as far back as 2000 BC the Egyptians were building walled gardens for protection against the elements; these gardens were pretty sophisticated, containing ponds to cool the air and date palms and sycamores for decoration and for plucking. The ancient Persians created gorgeous walled gardens with balanced, formal design—they were masters of the art, and their gardens provided order, calm, and sanctuary from the dust and relentless heat of the world outside. Fruit trees and flowers offered shade, colour, and scent; cascades, pools, and canals cooled the air and irrigated the plants. These gardens had a spiritual quality, offering a place for rest and contemplation.

Medieval monks also created serene walled gardens perfect for repose and religious contemplation. The monks believed that gardening itself was an act of healing, as I was discovering, and that just being in pleasant outdoor surroundings could "revive a dying spirit and soften the hardness of a mind," as the Cistercian monk Gilbert of Hoyland wrote in twelfth-century England. In many monasteries, monks who had been bled (as often as half a dozen times a year) were allowed to rest on cots in the infirmary garden to regain their strength. Bloodletting was thought to relieve the stresses of monkhood, but perhaps it was the week of rest in a fragrant, herb-filled garden that really did the trick.

I DIDN'T LOOK for rest in my new garden—the simple act of gardening was what I found beneficial. And I must have been doing something right—my tomatoes thrived, even if my sad little perimeter borders, with flowers planted side by side because the borders were too narrow to plant two deep, didn't measure up to Uncle Ren's thickly planted garden or even my mother-in-law's flowery but controlled borders.

But my tomatoes were red and juicy, tempting me to pluck one and eat it out of my hand every time I went out to pull a few weeds. Maybe they were responding to my loving care: following Ren's farmerly advice, I staked them with sturdy poles (from Ren's store of old broom handles), tying them with cotton strips (torn from my mom's old bedsheets); I kept the plants in bounds by pinching out the suckers that grew in the axils of the main stems and the side branches; I bought special tomato fertilizer and fed them every three weeks; and I cut off some of the foliage once the fruit was turning rosy so that the sun could make it red. I even gave the plants a dose of salts—Epsom salts, recommended by a garden expert I heard on the radio as a special boost to the fruit. (Uncle Ren hadn't heard of this one.) And I was lucky, too: the weather that first summer I seriously gardened was perfect, and my tomatoes didn't suffer from blight or leaf roll or blossom-end rot, something I've had to deal with almost every summer since, when I've had a garden.

Blossom-end rot pretty well describes the problem—dark, scabby patches spread over the bottom of the fruit, making it useless unless you trim off the good parts for a sauce. But it's easy enough to avoid once you know the cause of the problem. It's caused by wide fluctuations in the moisture level of the soil, from drought to downpour, say, or a too-heavy application from your hose after you've let the plants sit without watering for a week. The dry soil prevents the plant from taking up enough calcium to allow the fruit to mature properly, and it's common when plants grow rapidly early in the season then set fruit during dry weather. The solution is to water regularly throughout the season, evenly and deeply, and to use a mulch to keep the soil moist during dry spells.

But I was just a beginner and didn't learn about the proper culture of tomatoes till I'd been gardening for many years. In the meantime I was discovering the spiritual and therapeutic values of gardening on my own and the hard way, with strenuous work—which is probably what my stoic forebears would have suggested as a cure for what ailed me. But too often, in my non-gardening hours of the day—and when I wasn't actually having a panic attack—I felt pressured, isolated, and upset, trying to juggle responsibilities I wasn't sure I could handle. I didn't know what was the matter with me. But life went on regardless of my worries—within the next four years our two babies became four: a beautiful, hoped-for girl we named Suzanne, and then our little dumpling, Michael. And my garden kept growing.

CHAPTER 4

CROWDED GARDEN

· · · · ·

Along time ago a gardener much better than I will ever become said it takes half a lifetime to decide what to do with a garden and the other half to do it.

This was Gertrude Jekyll, the indomitable and influential garden designer and writer whose life spanned the last part of the 1800s and the early years of the 1900s and whose photographs—at least the ones I've seen of her—show a large, rather intimidating lady in a sweeping dress, sensible shoes, and an imposing hat. Frankly, I think Gertrude was also an optimist. I'm sure I'll run out of lifetime before I get done to my garden what I think needs doing. But I didn't think this way when I had the misguided confidence of youth. I took years to wake up to the idea that there's more to making a garden than growing pretty flowers in rows.

What success I did have in the early years was mostly due to Uncle Ren. In my original narrow borders and a later apostrophe-shaped island bed I planted the treasured pots and plastic bags of transplants he generously sent home with me when we went to visit my mom for a weekend—pink, blue, and purple Canterbury bells, Pacific Giant delphiniums (which have never thrived in my gardens—something to do with humidity, I think), big pink spotted foxgloves any vixen would be proud to wear, dwarf bearded iris in a stunning deep purple, which I'm proud to say I still grow because I've taken pieces of the tuberous root with me every time I've moved, and, of course, Ren's famous dinner-plate dahlias. He grew only large-flowered dahlias, with blooms six to ten inches across with multiple rows of petals, on plants sometimes nearly four feet tall. Some were classified as cactus varieties, and these had slightly shaggy, slightly tubular petals that curved and twisted; his others were called decorative, more formal in style with rounded or pointed petals alternating in regular rows. I liked the more casual cactus types best, and Ren blessed me every year with tubers he'd wintered over in Granny's cold cellar. These he passed on with written instructions:

1. Plant tubers six inches deep in open holes, with the small white buds on top. Cover green shoots with earth as they grow upward towards the light.
2. Pinch out one shoot to keep one strong main stem.
3. Be sure to stake before the plants get too big.
4. Nip out the side branches and side buds to get one big bloom.

I followed these instructions to the letter and had dahlias that knocked out the neighbours. I admit the plants were tall and stiff, and they looked like sentries standing by themselves at intervals down my skinny border. But the flowers were fabulous. My mother-in-law obviously coveted them, and so I rather grandly passed a few tubers along to her when I received my allotment from Ren the following spring.

Because of Ren's plants, my reputation as a gardener began to spread along the street. I'm ashamed to say that vanity set in, along with a sneaky deceit I couldn't admit even to myself: I found myself shamelessly taking credit for the unusual and beautiful specimens Uncle Ren provided. Well, I didn't actually come out and announce I'd grown the plants myself. It was more a sin of omission, as the Catholic Church would say.

But I wasn't totally dependent on Ren's plants. I also frequented the local nursery whenever Joe was paying a visit to buy more grass seed or fertilizer, and I discovered a few new favourites. Crackerjack marigolds in orange and yellow I liked best because their colour was so constant, bright, and cheerful. They grew taller than the tiny edging marigolds I'd known from Ren's garden, about two feet high, and they branched out well, so they filled out my little borders and made them look less sparse. I liked the marigolds for their look, but I didn't much like their pungent smell. Then I read somewhere that they kept bugs away from tomatoes, so I bookended the tomato bed with marigolds.

I also fell for a Blaze climbing rose in bloom in a fibre pot in the nursery, and I bought it to grow against the yellow brick garage; it bloomed prolifically for years, till long after I moved out, in rich, crimson puffs, and even though there are probably better cultivars around you can't persuade me Blaze isn't the best climbing rose for hardiness and show in a Canadian garden. But my real nursery find was the Gloriosa daisy, a lovely mahogany and gold specimen with flowers that ranged from four to sometimes nearly six inches across and bloomed and bloomed from midsummer till frost. A relative of the black-eyed Susan, it had a graceful but upright habit, with long stems that reached out to show their cheerful flower faces; the colour was perfectly suited

47

to the autumn tones in our living room, and they made a long-lasting cut flower too, when I allowed myself to cut them. But then, as now, I hated to raid the garden for in-house arrangements; I preferred to see them filling the spaces in my garden.

The Gloriosa daisies also became the talk of the neighbourhood and the envy of my mother-in-law, and I began to feel I'd invented them myself. I started to grow them from seed in my basement, planting them in flats or little pots in March for later transplanting to the garden. This process became more complicated than starting from seed had seemed in Uncle Ren's garden shed. I read a newspaper column that advised using only sterilized soil for starting seeds or risk the dreaded damping-off disease, in which young seedlings essentially keel over in a kind of botanical crib death, suddenly and inexplicably, in their cozy tray of earth in your warm and protected basement. So I did as the columnist suggested and baked the potting soil I bought at the nursery in foil pans in the oven, creating a heavy, disgusting bat-cave smell in the house that lasted for days. You can be sure I did that only once. Even the neighbour kids over to play with mine held their noses as they ran out the front door. Heaven knows what they told their mommies.

These days sterilized seed-starter mix that's designed for starting seeds indoors is easy to buy at the nursery. It's not only sterilized, but also so light (most are a mix of perlite, sand, and compost) that even I can carry an eighty-four-litre bag easily into the house and down to the basement. I have a sneaking suspicion that the soil I bought long ago was also sterilized and that I didn't have to go through the baking process, but so be it.

My Gloriosa daisies grew like weeds in pots on the windowsill under available light, something I'd consider a miracle today: to start seeds indoors these days I have a set of full-spectrum fluorescent tubes in the basement, which burn for fourteen hours a day in late winter to give the seedlings sufficient light. Later in the spring, once the Gloriosas had been repotted and were sporting a good growth of leaves, I gave some away proudly, to my mother-in-law, to my neighbours, and to Uncle Ren. At last I was able to return his favours, and it was especially rewarding when he seemed truly impressed with my newly acquired horticultural talents.

HERE'S ANOTHER bit of gardening wisdom from our friend Gertrude—something she wrote in *Colour Schemes for the Flower Garden* in 1921 (its fifth edition): "As the critical faculty becomes keener, so does the standard of aim rise higher; and, year by year, the desired point seems always to elude attainment."

I wouldn't have put it quite that way, but I know what she meant. So do all gardeners. Once you think you've got things just right and you're feeling as satisfied as a cat with his very own tin of tuna, discontent sets in. It happened to me about year four. Suddenly my garden looked inadequate. The tomato bed looked lonely and the side borders skimpy, not at all the big show of colour I'd had in my mind's eye. My desired point of attainment was definitely eluding me.

I went back to the garden magazines on my coffee table and returned to Uncle Ren's *Better Homes and Gardens Garden Book*, which he'd lent me and which I pored over almost every night after the kids were tucked in. All these publications were filled with gorgeous gardens: family gardens with patios and chaises, barbecues and plastic tables with umbrellas, plus play space for the children; spilling-over rock gardens; pretty pools with goldfish and waterfalls; and glorious beds of perennials so well planned the gardeners could boast of having something in bloom from spring till frost. This is no mean feat, I know today—landscapers I've met over the years tell me that planning for continuous bloom is probably the most difficult part of garden design.

We had some of these ingredients—the swing set and sandbox, set in a shady corner under a maple tree; a new flagstone patio in the sunny square between the garage and the house and protected by a board fence on the street side; the requisite picnic table and barbecue; my workmanlike tomato patch and the modest side borders. But nothing seemed to cohere. In the magazines, the gardens flowed beautifully from one area to another, linked together so cleverly I couldn't figure out how this harmony was achieved.

All at once, standing out in the backyard at noon on a summer day, when the side borders looked washed out and skimpier than ever in the blinding sun and the grass in the middle had faded to a dry beige, I had a brainwave. What I needed was a big, wide, gobsmacking flowerbed in the middle of the yard, no matter how much digging I had to do. Maybe this would pull all the elements together—at least it would dominate and draw the eye. So I dug an apostrophe-shaped bed in the middle of the back lawn, a good, big one you couldn't miss as soon as you stepped onto the patio.

I jammed it with a patchwork of annuals and perennials. It was emphatic enough, but it didn't do the trick—it floated like an orphan in the grass and had no overall impact because of its wild mixture of colours. After a couple of summers I was woman enough to admit it did nothing for the garden as a whole, and I enlarged it into a seven-foot-wide rectangular border tucked up against the stone patio.

Doing so helped integrate the overall design, but I wasn't sure how to plant this larger bed. "In a big space like this, you don't want to plant in rows or in single plants," Ren advised. "Plant in big patches, with several of the same plant in each patch.

Then repeat the patches." I personally felt that to place plants in groups would waste their beauty. They would show themselves off better scattered singly throughout the border.

Ren, good teacher that he was, didn't press his point but let me learn on my own. It took me an eternity to wrap my mind around the concept of planting in drifts, which is how planting in patches is fashionably known today, and it happened by chance: in my third and present garden about fifteen years ago I had to move a perennial bed quickly, just before a backhoe destroyed it for a house extension, and I plunked all the perennials in a temporary bed in groups of the same variety so that I'd be able to identify them. The next spring I didn't have time to move them, and they looked better than they ever had, blooming en masse, five or six of the kind together. Could I be a slow learner?

Horticultural snobbery is, I think, a characteristic of young gardeners. It's like wanting plain hard-twist broadloom because your parents have oriental-style area rugs, or refusing to like your parents' music; come to think of it, it's akin to cutting the umbilical cord. In my early years I rejected not just much of Uncle Ren's advice (I didn't reject his plants, as you've noticed) but also many old-fashioned garden favourites. I refused to grow bleeding heart or spirea, King Alfred daffodils or ordinary red tulips. Instead I gravitated towards less common dogwood and quince, Thalia narcissus and the new Red Emperor tulips. I scorned petunias, ignored alyssum, and rejected day lilies. Since those callow days I've learned to appreciate the value of standard, garden-variety plants. They may not be glamorously new, but they are dependably hardy and often disease resistant, and they offer solid bloom.

ACTUALLY, I'VE wondered many times whether my need for individuality and control of my own space, combined with the fenced-in life I was leading as a round-the-clock mother and wife isolated in the 'burbs with similar women who (unlike me) seemed to be managing beautifully, contributed to my emotional state. I certainly felt confined by more than my panic attacks. I had no money of my own to spend and no mobility, since the suburban bus service was inadequate and I couldn't drive. Joe wouldn't allow it: he needed the car for work, but there was more to his refusal than that. His vehicles were always a serious part of his identity, his pride and joy. He bought a shiny new convertible every other year, no matter what the state of our finances (although I knew little of that situation) and always kept his cars in pristine condition. It took three or four years after our move to the suburbs to convince him (aided by his parents) that I needed to be able to drive in case of an emergency. We presented what seemed to me even then as superficial arguments: if he became ill, how would we get him to the hospital, or how would I buy groceries? But even after I got my licence he allowed me little access to the car. Occasionally when I persuaded him I needed to go to the plaza after supper to test my driving chops I'd find him pacing the driveway when I got home. I persevered, however, and found that driving gave me a feeling of independence; years later I was even able to have my own car.

Despite the satisfaction and pride I continued to glean from gardening and other rewarding tasks—I actually liked making the house shine and experimenting with new recipes, although I wished my family, including my spouse, wouldn't say "*Eeeyuu...*" every time I put something different on the table— my panic attacks and general symptoms of anxiety still appeared with regularity. They'd almost seemed to become a habit. My family doctor was sympathetic and as helpful as he could be, offering counselling and prescriptions for the latest tranquillizers, but I was on a treadmill that kept going faster. Finally, after a particularly disturbing development, and much to my relief, he suggested I "see someone," as if he were afraid the suggestion was so shameful he couldn't utter the word psychiatrist. Or was I misreading him? He probably thought I was ashamed of my teetering emotions and was trying to be gentle. The funny thing is that I was reticent about suggesting myself that I transfer to a shrink because I didn't want to hurt *his* feelings.

I gladly embraced the therapy; thus began a couple of years of outpourings in which I examined every corner of my life while the doctor said virtually nothing. Well, as any patient of psychotherapy will tell you, he did nod now and then and ask leading questions. Many of them led me down revealing paths through my life, my psyche, and my marriage and sent me home exhausted, where I'd close the bedroom door and lie down so that I could mull things over further.

I know now that I had a classic case of agoraphobia, although no one used that word then—did it even exist? I was probably predisposed to it, in some part by the death of my father; it was clearly triggered by the birth of my first baby and compounded by my own shaky confidence as a new mother, as well as my isolation in the suburbs. Agoraphobia is a riddle even to the medical profession. I never spoke about my panic attacks even to my closest friends. No one spoke of such things. I simply avoided the occasions and places that might provoke an attack, which increasingly seemed to be almost everywhere except my own backyard.

Sometimes the panic would begin with a simple feeling of unease, which might start as I sat in a crowded room that was warmer than usual. It might begin when I was left alone, such as after Joe went to work in the morning. I'd begin to feel vaguely anxious. My breathing would become shallow, and I'd develop a tightness in my chest or a lump in my throat. I might feel numb

53

in some part of my body, or twenty feet tall and swaying, or separated from the world, looking down on people and situations as if they were happening somewhere else. If I was outside, the wind might swirl threateningly around my ears and make me dizzy. My brain would race, out of control, a swirl of images and thoughts of drastic outcomes. My abdomen would contract, giving me extreme cramps. My heart would race uncontrollably. I'd try slow breathing to control it, but panic had taken hold. Was I having a heart attack? Was I going to die? Was I going to kill myself?

For a short period I was unable to eat. I'd make dinner for my family and sit down feeling hungry, and suddenly my mouth felt filled with dust. I could hardly swallow, let alone chew food. This really scared me, and it was this troubling incident that sent me to the shrink.

Feelings like these must seem ludicrous to someone who's never experienced them, but they are very real to one who has.

EVEN THOUGH gardening was not a competitive sport in our neighbourhood, I developed a rival down the street. She followed her family tradition of English gardening, whereas I didn't think I was gardening in any particular style. In the beginning I followed Uncle Ren's lead, then I began to pick up the styles set out in garden books and magazines. Of course I had no knowledge of gardening history at the time; I'd never heard of Gertrude Jekyll, that doyenne of early-twentieth-century garden styles, nor did I know anything abut Thomas Church, the contemporary California landscape architect whose ideas were reflected in the publications I was reading. He believed that gardens should be an extension of the home, with functional areas set in an overall plan and with texture and colour in the form of indigenous flora.

My rival's house was the same plan as mine, with a separate garage connected to the house by a long board fence. Her sunny square between them was a carpet of cool green grass, and over the garage tumbled an erotic mass of Blaze, which I considered *my* rose. Worse, she had a spectacular six-foot-wide perennial border filled with gorgeous classics and new cultivars that I couldn't look at lest envy overtake me. The only thing that comforted me was that her garden looked like a lawn containing a bed of flowers, not like the integrated gardens in magazines.

We became friends because our kids played together, and soon we were swapping plants and gardening and cooking tips. We discovered we shared a desire to garden in the front as well as the back, an unknown concept in those days of front lawns as far as the eye could see. She persuaded her husband to dig her a good-sized bed in the front, and he accommodated with a six-by-four-foot plot on the grass beside the driveway. All it lacked was a tombstone.

"It may turn out to be his grave," she commented to me through gritted teeth, but she planted it all the same with colourful annuals. Eventually it became an island of shrubs, and later it disappeared altogether.

My front-yard effort was a long foot-wide strip on the grassy space between our driveway and the next-door neighbours' that went from just in front of our garage right down to the road. Frankly, it looked even punier than my narrow back borders had, but I had to keep this border narrow because half the width of the strip belonged to the neighbours, and they preferred grass. In this strip I broke down and planted the petunias I usually scorned because I realized they'd provide colour all summer and into fall, but I chose the cascading kind because they would stay low and spill over the edges of the border. The line of almost solid colour was like a peachy pink ribbon tossed down beside the driveway,

55

and I had to admit the petunias worked well, despite their plebeian family background. Even petunias have their place.

Once the border was in bloom the neighbours came around a bit and agreed the stark driveway area benefited with a little softening. Then they also agreed to share with us the cost of planting a trio of Austrian pines at the top end of the strip, for a little shade and front-entrance privacy for both of us. This move was one we should never have made. Because they worked so well as a windbreak, the sturdy Austrian pines were favourites of highway planners at the time, and they looked so graceful around the cloverleafs we decided they would add some personality to our garden. Ours were cute little trees when we put them in, but in twenty years they had engulfed the driveways and had to be limbed up; they retaliated by dripping sap over any car so audacious as to park beneath them.

As the years passed and my gardening confidence grew, I stopped letting people think that I had cleverly raised from seed all the unique cultivars that had actually passed from Ren's garden to mine. "Oh, that one," I'd say. "That's a chrysanthemum from my uncle's garden. He's a great gardener and probably gave me half of what I grow here."

I also allowed Joe to hire a landscape company to design a new entrance planting. This was a milestone because I'd always felt the gardens were my territory, even if he was in charge of the lawn. The new planting was a conversation piece, actually: a sophisticated grouping of dwarf mugo pines, which reminded me of green cushions, around a concrete Japanese lantern set in a bed of gravel and river stones, the whole delineated by a low boxwood hedge. Very oriental, very serene. It added a unique element to my otherwise typically suburban flower garden, and I adopted it wholeheartedly.

My garden was changing and maturing, and so was I. The garden still pleased me, but I realized I was spending too much of my time pleasing others. Yet no one seemed to care who I was. My weekly sessions with the shrink moved to monthly visits, and then I graduated from therapy altogether, although if a panic attack raised its ugly head, which still happened now and again, or if I was especially troubled about something, I'd pay him a visit. I was ashamed of my lingering panic attacks and suspected I had also developed a reputation as a snob, or at least as an antisocial neurotic. But I knew my real nature was not antisocial—I liked being with people, even crowds of them—so it was important to develop some way of dealing with my attacks, even if they were less frequent. I always hated myself if I refused to go on an outing because I feared what might happen.

On my own, I had developed a kind of desensitization technique. Before going to the movies, for example, I'd promise myself that I had to stay for only twenty minutes; longer than that and I deserved a medal. I'd be sure to get an aisle seat close to the back, and if the uncomfortable feelings began I'd rise quickly and stand at the back. A few times I spent half the movie there, but because I didn't feel trapped and at the mercy of my rising fear, I could conquer the panic. Sometimes I even forgot myself and became caught up in the movie; then I'd slip into a rear seat for the rest of the show.

This technique began to work with almost everything— elevators, parties, concerts, supermarkets, neighbourhood kaffeklatches. (Strangely enough, I never felt panic when I was out in the car.) No one noticed if I left early because I always had a logical reason, but I stayed longer and longer. As I gained more and more control and understanding of my anxieties, a process that took the better part of a decade, I also developed a mental exercise I called onion peeling, wherein I'd mentally strip away the layers of an anxiety I was facing down until it was revealed to have nothing at its centre.

Unfortunately, I began to onion peel my marriage, too, and found there was little at its centre. Now that the kids were growing up and I was feeling better, I longed to find a real job more challenging than the volunteer hospital work I was doing. It had been a valuable learning experience as well as a confidence booster and had led to a small paid assignment writing a community column for the local weekly newspaper in Mississauga, Ontario, where we lived. But as far as Joe was concerned, there would be no discussion of any paying job. I belonged at home.

We had never argued much, and maybe that was a problem. We'd both come from homes where raised voices were seldom heard, and although they made for stress-free childhoods we probably got married with unrealistic views of how a good relationship should work. If we had a problem, we stepped around it. As I'd got further into therapy I'd begun to realized how much I resented his assumption that because I was the wife my wishes, and my desire to expand and develop whatever talents I had, came second. Therapy may have forced me to recognize my feelings, but when I worked up the courage to discuss them with Joe, he'd reject them, and I'd knuckle under. My emotions were my problem, he said, not his, and it was up to me to come to terms with my unhappiness. "You've changed!" he shouted at me once when I tried to open up yet another job discussion. "You're not the girl I married! What's *wrong* with you?"

He was right—I had changed. He was also right about something else: I was going to have to come to terms with my own unhappiness. To some degree I had learned to deal with my feelings of frustration by almost enjoying them. As the doctor had suggested in a rare moment of direct comment, I was in danger of becoming a martyr to my disorder. But how was I to reverse this tendency, to completely heal myself and come to terms with my marriage, if my husband wouldn't discuss our problems? Would that ever happen?

But that, of course, is only my side of the story.

One spring while I was planting the front-yard strip, something happened that struck me as portentous: my wedding ring slipped off and disappeared into the depths of the earth. I noticed it was gone as soon as I went into the house, but although I searched the areas where I'd been digging, it didn't appear. The reason I know it fell in exactly that spot is that I found the ring again a couple of years later, while I was putting in fall bulbs. This story would be positive if it foretold a happy ending—a found ring, a mended psyche, a healed marriage—but by the time I lost the ring it was too late for a ride into the sunset.

The next year I somehow found the courage to move out, with no job and little money. I was leaving home again to find myself, just as I'd done twenty-five years earlier when I was sixteen, but this time I severed an important tie forever and left some valuables behind: my children, who were past childhood but still needed the security of a family unit. My unilateral departure (some could call it selfish, and some did) may have turned out all right for me, but it left heartaches all around that will never heal.

CHAPTER 5

Green
ONIONS RETURN

. . . . .

"ARE YOU SURE this is the right thing to do?" Mom had asked me anxiously when I told her I was leaving Joe. I knew she and my in-laws had conferred a couple of times about the sorry state of our marriage, but like good parents they had not interfered. Sometimes I wished they had—I could have used a little emotional support, or even a good talking to, during the darkest of my days. I could understand my mom's concern; separation and divorce were unheard of in our family and uncommon among my contemporaries, even in the early '70s, when I moved out. Worse yet, I had no job and would have no financial support—Joe was wild about my departure, and after a few attempts at persuading me to come back, as long as I would promise to try harder to make things work, he abandoned the idea, and me. He hasn't spoken to me since.

My children suffered, too, since I had to leave them as well as him, and how my actions affected them even though we maintained as much closeness as we could has left a permanent ache in my heart.

As for me, the stars must have been perfectly aligned. Within a month of my leaving home my small job as a community columnist led magically to a full-time job on its sister weekly in Oakville, the adjoining town; there I threw myself into reporting, writing, and editing, and even taking photos when it was my weekend to work. I learned the basics of editing and writing on that job, and on the job I also met the publication's sports editor, a man several years my junior but on my wavelength; his name was Chris, and I felt as if I'd known him for years. We conversed effortlessly, and his dry humour struck a chord with me; somehow it kept my worries in perspective. Chris and I became close companions, and when he decided to take a new position in Montreal within the year, it seemed natural for me to go with him.

But have I completely taken leave of my senses? I asked myself the question I'm sure my friends and family were asking each other. Leaving a job I was lucky to have and children who needed me reasonably close at hand to live with a man I'd known for less than a year didn't seem like a good idea, to say the least. So I took it a step at a time. First, I took a trip to Montreal to see if there were any jobs I might qualify for. And here the stars were with me once again: *Weekend Magazine,* a weekly publication delivered with the Saturday papers across Canada, had just advertised for a copy editor. The chief copy editor liked my varied experience on a weekly newspaper—short-lived as it was—and she liked me; I got the job even though I probably wasn't as qualified as some of the new journalism graduates she interviewed, but I seemed to hold the edge in hands-on experience and maturity. I couldn't believe my luck. Then, second, Chris found a spacious third-floor apartment, with an extra bedroom for visiting children, at an incredibly low price. A promising job and comfortable digs, both discovered on one reconnoitering visit! I figured fate was definitely trying to tell me something, and I took the plunge.

Gardening, of course, was hardly a priority for the three years we lived in Montreal. Except for boxes of annuals and a few herbs on our apartment balcony, it was put on hold for a few years as I tended to more important challenges: building a career and loving every hard-working minute of it, and maintaining a long-distance relationship with my children. We managed monthly visits, usually with me returning to Mississauga, where they lived with their father, but occasionally they would come to stay with us.

Three years later good fortune intervened again when *Weekend* decided it needed another senior editor in the Toronto office, and I was given the job. It was a promotion, and it meant a transfer back to Toronto. I was delirious. The years in Montreal had been positive for Chris and me, we'd both honed our skills, and we'd developed a solid relationship more mature than my marriage had ever been, so there was no question about Chris returning with me (we eventually married, but our progress deserves more than an aside, and I shall elaborate upon it later).

We rented an old farmhouse in Mississauga not too far from where my children lived. The white clapboard house was an anachronism among the modern homes around it, but it was a homey little place, and it had a small yard that was formerly farmland. I eyed the rich, dark earth, yearning to scratch my gardening itch once again.

Our landlords, who lived next door in a new house built on a lot severed from the original farm, were keen gardeners, although vegetables, not ornamental flowers, were their specialty. The first summer we were there I broached the subject of a garden, but I realized from the glances they exchanged that they thought we were career people who'd probably never held a trowel and would lose interest at the sight of the first weed. "Maybe next year; it's too late now, anyway," the landlord said gruffly.

Having your landlord living a stone's throw from your front door is an advantage when the drains back up or the power fails but not when you're trying to live your life. But we paid our rent on time and didn't give noisy parties, and apparently their not-so-clandestine surveillance convinced them we were worthy of a garden. The next spring the landlord offered a big square of fertile earth next to his vegetable patch, and he agreed that I could dig up the bit of lawn between the side entrance of our house and the driveway to plant flowers. Yippee! I was back in business.

In a fit of enthusiasm I grew copious amounts of vegetables, many more than Chris and I could possibly consume. The rich earth and the warm sun that fell on this lovely spot nurtured the vegetables, and they thrived like none I'd seen before. They looked lusher and more productive than my recollections of the produce in my dad's garden or of anything Ren had grown. I couldn't believe my beginner's luck.

Of course I had green onions, but they mainly went into salads; only a few were sneaked between slabs of white bread smeared with mayo, in honour of my childhood. I grew the best green beans ever, the French *haricots verts*, because I'd eaten them in restaurants and could almost never buy them in markets, and I tried fava beans, which were a miserable failure. Tomatoes? Naturally—the big beefsteaks I'd grown earlier were everybody's favourite. Common sweet basil, the best variety to eat with tomatoes, and lettuces of several kinds except for iceberg, which had become frowned upon because it was said to have no taste or nutritional value. It was all we ate when I was a kid and later, when I was cooking for my family, and I agree about the taste, but I still wonder about reports of its lack of vitamins. Buttery Boston or green and red leaf lettuces were by then *de rigueur*, and something "new" called mesclun—a mix of mustard greens, arugula, chicory, and more—which had its origins in French cuisine, picked when the leaves were two inches high and doused with extra-virgin olive oil, white wine vinegar and salt.

I wasn't sure enough of my vegetable-growing skill to try the new mesclun greens yet, although once tried they proved no more difficult than any other vegetables, but the regular leaf lettuces were a success. Like all plants, they wanted to grow and they did, given the right conditions, which this little plot had. I realized early that the best way to achieve success with any leaf lettuce was to pick it as often as it sprouted leaves large enough to drop into a salad or on your sandwich. New ones would grow in a week or so. The worst thing to do was leave them alone, then they'd go to seed—or bolt, as my landlord described it. The word brought to mind a ridiculous image of lettuces dashing to a finish line, and I guess the image was accurate enough— they would, after all, be rushing to fulfill their seed-producing destiny. But by that time the leaves would be bitter and strong, definitely not salad material.

The same pick-'em-young philosophy applied to the *haricots verts*, which some cynic told me were just plain old green beans with French attitude. I laughed when he said it, but I thought the comment was unfair. These were special beans! Sometimes called French filet beans, they are the official bean of salade niçoise and they know it: they're small and slender (hey, they're French, aren't they?), with an intense flavour. And they're stringless, although most green or string beans are bred today without the string you once had to pull out from between the two halves of the pod. I picked my *haricots verts* about every three days, ideally when they were a tetch bigger than the tines of a large dinner fork. If you leave them till they grow too big they'll be tough. They're best popped into boiling water within a minute of picking and cooked for no more than a minute, then drained and dressed with a bit of butter or olive oil and salt.

Fava beans, which have been domesticated for thousands of years and are often used as a cover crop, dug into the soil to enrich it with nitrogen (they're related to the legume family), have become one of my favourite vegetables, although in my family I seem to be alone in appreciating them. But I won't try growing them again. They get too tall—some varieties reach six feet—and require staking, and they have unattractive leaves (to my mind, anyway) that tend to dry and crack. They have to be planted very early in spring because they don't like hot weather, and they aren't prolific bearers. Those are enough reasons to buy instead of grow them, and I seek them out at farmers' markets in the spring, while they're still fresh and young.

Simple preparation is best with favas, too, but you have to parboil them (after you've released them from their furry little beds inside the pods) and slip them out of their tough outer skins after you've chilled them in a cold water bath for a few minutes. I like them for breakfast prepared as follows, with a few slices of basil-sprinkled tomatoes on the side: For a couple of cups of podded and skinned beans, lightly sweat two sliced green onions in a half cup of extra-virgin olive oil in a medium saucepan. Add the prepared beans to the saucepan, and then add water or chicken stock to just cover the beans. Simmer till the liquid disappears and the beans are tender, about twenty minutes, maybe less. Add a good pinch of coarse sea salt and the juice of a lemon (or less to taste). Yum. A purée of fava beans is also delicious and different served with a platter of crudités: purée cooked beans with a good douse of extra-virgin olive oil, a couple of cloves of roasted garlic, salt and lemon juice to taste. Add the lemon juice a half-teaspoon at a time and keep tasting: the beans benefit from a lift of lemon, but too much overpowers the purée and makes it acidic. If the purée is too thick, add a few drops of cooking liquid or more oil, and lots more garlic if you like it as much as I do.

65

While I was furiously digging my new vegetable bed, planting seeds in careful rows like my dad's, weeding and then harvesting in the hot days of that summer, I never stopped to ask myself why I was so suddenly gung ho about growing vegetables. Maybe down deep I realized I might never have this combination of circumstances again—the weatherman's promise of a perfect summer and a flat plot of rich, productive earth in a protected spot in full sun. How could a gardener say no? I might have been fulfilling my destiny or answering the call of a cultural imperative: the compelling influence of my dad's Victory Garden and the farm gardens grown by Uncle Ren and all my other uncles and aunts, where they raised food to feed their families and the hired hands, as well as to sell or store for winter.

I don't know how many hired hands and family members Henry David Thoreau had to feed from his garden, but he grew rows of beans that totalled *seven miles*. I suspect there was more than a little gardening DNA in his makeup and maybe a shred or two of compulsion—here's something he wrote in *Walden:* "What was the meaning of this... small Herculean labour, I know not. I came to love my rows, my beans, though so many more than I wanted. They attached me to the earth... But why should I raise them? Only heaven knows."

In my travels I've noticed the same compulsion among retired Prairies farm couples who've left the land and taken up residence in town. Even though all the kids have grown up and left home and only the two of them live in the new bungalow, they turn over the whole backyard to a gigantic vegetable garden: potatoes, corn, carrots, beets, broccoli, cabbage, squash (all of which are easier to come by at the market), tomatoes, onions, lettuce, cucumbers, planted in regimented rows. When I've asked what on earth they do with the harvest, they invariably reply that most of it goes to their children (who may have farms

66

and vegetable gardens of their own) or into preserving jars and the freezer for winter.

But although these good Canadian gardens are repositories of nutrition and evidence of a strong and constant work ethic, for elaborate design they don't measure up to the gardens of wealthy European landowners in the sixteenth century. Their vegetable gardens were arranged in formal patterns, following the prevailing style of ornamental gardening. Geometric in shape and containing traditional varieties as well as "exotic" (for the time) vegetables like potatoes, eggplants, tomatoes, and pumpkins brought back from the New World by explorers, the beds were separated by brick or gravel pathways and bordered with evergreen herbs such as lavender, rosemary, or santolina. Sometimes the edging plants were combined to create the illusion of interwoven ribbons of green and grey, and they became known as knot gardens. The vegetables themselves were integral to the design and were planted in mosaics of texture and colour, and the gardens were dressed up with twiggy teepees for holding pole beans, fruit tunnels, topiaries, and espaliers against the outer wall. They were great places for strolling as well as picking vegetables for supper.

The most extravagant of all the fancy vegetable gardens was the *potager du Roi* at Versailles in France, made for Louis XIV, the Sun King, in 1683; it ran to twenty-three acres, but then Louis had three thousand mouths to feed at the palace. He loved to eat as well, and in addition to the mountains of carrots and beans and cabbages and leeks and gooseberries, cherries and pears, and hundreds of other species that his gardeners grew, he demanded they deliver fresh salad greens and his favourite asparagus to his table in January. They achieved this by growing the plants under fresh, warm manure, I trust with some kind of separation between protector and protectee. Otherwise, those little green stalks would require a serious bath. Running a close second to Versailles but more believable as a real vegetable garden at about an acre in size is Château de Villandry, in France's Loire Valley. It was created in the Middle Ages by monks who planted their produce in a grid of nine squares, with vegetables and flowers chosen for their colour and texture planted in complex mosaic patterns. Both these grand potagers have been restored as faithfully as possible to their former appearance and are open for public strolling, although they're not for picking.

If I should ever move to a large property in the country and have the space to grow a vegetable garden again, I'll design mine like a potager because it would be a living reminder that growing food need not be strictly utilitarian. But mine will be more along the lines of Rosemary Verey's twentieth-century potager in her garden at Barnsley House in Gloucestershire, England. Poor Rosemary is gone, but her garden lives on, rooted in the historical style, with squares of colourful vegetables artfully combined—Boston lettuces grown beside the architectural points of single leeks, for example—and the squares are separated with flat stone pathways and outlined with mounding evergreen plants. But it has an exuberant, natural feeling that would make any monk or modern woman happy and content while digging, weeding, or planting veggies.

WE LIVED IN the little white farmhouse for only two summers, and I gardened seriously there for only one, but as I write about it I realize it was important to me in many ways. It signified a return to my natural life, my life outside my newly budding career, and the time marked my realization that my panic attacks had disappeared. One morning, while climbing onto the crowded commuter train to my job in the city, it struck me that I hadn't even thought about panic attacks for years. I couldn't remember the last time that awful feeling had shaken my equilibrium. More telling, Mom told me that one day Uncle Ren had commented that I seemed like my old self again, the me who'd been around in the early days.

There was something more—a small milestone I didn't realize at the time: the seed of a serious desire for a front-yard garden was starting to germinate. Of course it wouldn't sprout above the earth for years, until well after we'd moved into our own house and I'd gardened long enough there that I'd run out of space in the back, but the idea took root in that little space between the driveway and the door to the house the landlord allowed my to dig up. I'd spent a couple of hot afternoons digging out the sod and turning over the soil, then I'd filled the plot with spires of Blue Victoire salvia and coral verbena. I planted closely for thick growth and a good show, wishing I could put in perennials but knowing we wouldn't be there for a long time and annuals were more practical.

That bed was spectacular in its own small way. It greeted us brightly at the end of a working day, and it bounced and nodded colourfully in the breeze outside the big kitchen window, beckoning to us as we sat at our new harvest table eating supper every night. The bed added cheer and personality to the little white clapboard farmhouse, although I suspected our landlords didn't see it that way. I really think they felt the dooryard was a place for grass, not gaudy flowers.

I had also fallen out of favour with the landlord, an unforgiving man. I hadn't picked my beans fast enough, and by the end of the season he was complaining that too many were going to seed on the bush. Some of the lettuce had bolted. The next spring he announced that he was sorry, but I could no longer have a section of his garden to grow vegetables. By that time it no longer mattered to me—we had decided we could afford to buy a house of our own.

CHAPTER 6

❦

Seasons Come

AND SEASONS GO

. . . . .

OUR NEW HOUSE looked as though it had escaped from a
Monopoly game: a little red brick box with a steeply
pitched roof, a door in the middle and a window on each
side. I don't mean to poke fun at it; it was, and is, a cute, cot-
tagey kind of house in a friendly suburban neighbourhood of
curving streets, about a mile from my former home in Mississauga (where my kids still lived, although they were back and
forth to college or university). Our house was just right for two
people and maybe a couple of house guests now and then. It also
sat on a large lot—65 by 130 feet—of mainly grass, the perfect
canvas for an ambitious gardener.

The plantings we inherited were typical of the others in our
subdivision, which the developers preferred to call a "planned
community" when it was built in the early 1950s, about the same
time as my former neighbourhood. I swear most of the trees and
shrubs had been planted by the original owners, except for the
three even older apple trees. They were relics of the original

turn-of-the century orchard on which our houses were built—
yes, just like the place where my first garden grew, although not
the same orchard. And to honour its provenance, all the streets
in our development had been named for apple varieties—Rus-
sett, Courtland, Melba, McIntosh. There was a McIntosh tree
in the middle of this front lawn, too, and two other not easily
identified varieties in the back, set about twenty feet apart, as
they're planted in orchards. They were lovely beings with their
own personalities, and that's in the past tense because they're
sadly gone now, victims of old age, although they kept bearing
right up till the end, as good apple trees do.

The usual pair of overgrown Skyrocket junipers on each side
of the entrance jostled to get through the front door, and another
stood like a huge sentry at one corner of the house. A couple of
privets with bare legs and a not-so-dwarf spruce gawked into
the living room through the lone picture window, which had
been one of the builder's selling points twenty-five years earlier. In the back, a line of flowering shrubs marched around the
perimeter of the backyard—relatively young ones put in by the
owner we bought from—and a row of cedars and an exceedingly overgrown Pfitzer juniper separated our yard near the
house from the one next door and flopped over the patio outside the kitchen door. A large Norway maple threw dense shade
into the left quadrant of the backyard. We thought it was fully
grown, but it's added at least fifteen feet in height and breadth
over the years since we moved in. I've had a love-hate relationship with that tree ever since.

Chris and I took possession of our house in July 1978, leaving little time for a garden the first year, except to dig out those
trespassing Skyrocket junipers and trim back some of the nosy
foliage under the picture window. But we had plenty to do
inside—Michael earned pocket money by painting the walls

and kitchen cupboards as we soaked off wallpaper in some of the rooms. I had also taken a more challenging position handling some of the special publications, including the restaurant and food guide, at *Toronto Life* magazine, so I spent my dishwashing time at home staring out the window over the kitchen sink and planning what I'd do in the garden the next year. I suppose it was my first lesson in observing my space so that I could assess the changing light and shade, its windy and calm spots, the places where the frost disappears first in spring—its microclimates, as gardeners like to say.

The next spring, encouraged by my success in the rental garden, I dug a second vegetable bed, in the right rear quadrant of the yard opposite the Norway maple and just out of reach of its shady fingers. The sunniest spot was actually the middle of the yard, but it was mainly occupied by our senior citizen the Melba apple. That's what Chris concluded it was after a bit of research into old varieties. It bore abundantly the first autumn we were in our house—and many autumns thereafter—bestowing upon us bushels of crisp, tart apples perfect for pies. I made so many pies and jars of applesauce we had to buy a large freezer to store what the kids refused to take with them, and Chris became an expert baker of apple bars, turning out dozens of them. I still can't face them. The freezer came fully into its own after we harvested the crop from the vegetable garden.

It wasn't as successful as the one in the rental garden because conditions weren't perfect. Our garden simply had more shade than was ideal, and the roots of that blasted Norway maple extended much farther than its canopy and interfered with some of my vegetables. But I grew strawberries, a row each of broccoli and carrots, three rows of beans (this time I tried Blue Lake because Mom said they were the best) and many herbs as edging, including plenty of basil to go with the twenty-four tomato plants. Yes, twenty-four—for two people. I was obsessed. It was a good summer for tomatoes, and the fruit grew to dimensions I hadn't seen before and to heights of sweet juiciness I hadn't tasted in my previous tomato patches. I ate tomatoes three times a day, made sauce for the freezer and gave away *bushels*.

I also tucked in a few tomatillo plants, which we'd tasted on a trip to Mexico. I thought they might be too tender for our climate, but how wrong I was. They were annuals, after all, and would grow anywhere there was sun and warmth. The plants thrived, widely branched specimens with many little green tomatolike fruits encased in papery husks. They aren't related to tomatoes at all, bearing a closer relationship to the cape gooseberry, and they have a tangy yet sweetish taste and are often used for salsas in Central America. I harvested hundreds and then wondered what to do with them. I made soup and salsas and a pretty good pasta sauce of my own invention, some of which was passed along to my son Joe, who had his little downtown flat by this time, and to Suzy, who was living in an apartment on campus. Joe confessed later that he threw most of his out, but Suzy—who'd always had an adventurous palate—dutifully complimented me on its zesty, unusual taste. The real problem with tomatillos is that they reseed wantonly—they were interesting visitors for a time, but I had to become rude and kick them out when they spread into the flowerbeds in ensuing years.

That summer was my first encounter with the tomato horn-worm, and I trust it will be my last with these beasts. In my opinion it's the scariest insect in the world. But I guess everyone has a bug story to tell. Mom used to describe with colourful imagery (she'd been an English teacher) the clouds of grasshoppers—or was it a plague of locusts?—that darkened Prairie skies during the Depression, destroying crops and sending most of the population to the poorhouse. A friend of mine still fairly shivers in horror when she describes the heaving piles of June bugs swept up against the curb at the local supermarket way back in the summer of '57. Another friend looks positively ill when she talks about earthworms and how they wait for her on the sidewalk after a rain, grinning malevolently. Being a serious gardener who fears earthworms is no fun, but she's solved the problem by never putting her hands in the earth without the protection of a good pair of gardening gloves.

But this tomato hornworm nearly made me quit gardening. One morning I went to inspect the twenty-four tomato plants, which had been perfectly healthy the evening before, and found a couple of them nearly stripped of leaves. As I drew closer I saw what I thought was a rolled up leaf in the crook of a stem and the main stalk. I touched it, and my blood ran cold. It wasn't a leaf but a green and white monster, a fat thing at least four inches long and with a red horn at one end. I swear it hissed at me. Alerted by my bloodcurdling scream, Chris rushed to my rescue with the shovel and chopped the beast to bits in about ten minutes. It exuded green slime, and I couldn't help but think of *Invasion of the Body Snatchers*, which up to then had been my favourite sci-fi movie.

I had a second hornworm incident that summer, but this time there was no man around to help me. So I ran into the house and grabbled the killer insect spray. I sprayed clouds of it on the intruder and was dismayed as it writhed in apparent agony for several minutes before it died, its movements so powerful that the tomato plant swayed back and forth. I was horrified at the pain I'd caused a poor creature who was just eating to survive and fled to the house in tears.

I felt even worse when I found out that the tomato hornworm metamorphoses into a handsome grey-brown moth with an orange-yellow spotted body. It's known as the sphinx or

butterfly moth because of its habit of hovering as it drinks nectar from a flower. But it's as huge as its larva—about four inches
in wing span—so it would probably scare me, too.

ALTHOUGH I GREW out of my vegetable-gardening phase the
next year, I did adopt a practice during my farmer period that
I've never given up and never will. And that's composting.

Composting is nature. Composting is sometimes a stinky
manure pile, like on my uncles' farms. Composting is plants
dying and returning to the earth to feed it and support future
growth. Composting is what will happen to all of us eventually,
even if we choose to be cremated and our ashes thrown to the
winds. Come to think of it, cremation is a faster type of composting. I joke with my family on occasion that after I'm gone
I'd like to have my ashes scattered over my tomatoes, presum-
ing I'm still growing them. I'm rather hoping they take me seriously, although they look at me sideways when I say that. Do
they think it's a macabre idea?

But why not? I heard of a woman a few streets from me, a
lifelong serious gardener, whose family asked the new owner
of her house after she died if her ashes could be sprinkled over
her old garden. The new owner thought it was a fine idea, and
I imagine this woman's spirit overseeing the growth of the new
owner's plants. I once paid a visit to this garden, and I must say
it had a serene, almost spiritual air.

Composting wasn't a practice among city gardeners during the early '80s because recycling wasn't the popular habit it
is today, so those tidy brown plastic composting bins weren't
being distributed by the municipality, nor were they sold at any
garden supply company of my acquaintance. To compost you
did it the farmer's manure-pile way, or you built your own bin.
I chose the farmer's method (sans the horseshit, of course) and

dug a shallow pit in the far corner of the vegetable bed, next to the white picket fence that marked the boundary between our property and the three adjoining ones. It was fall, so I put a thick layer of chopped-up leaves from that abundant Norway maple in the bottom and then some of the earth I'd dug out and started filling the hole with vegetable peelings and crushed egg shells and so on from the kitchen, plus grass clippings and prunings from the garden. I followed all the rules, never putting in meat bits or bones or leftover rinds of cheese, and I added a thin layer of soil and chopped leaves every so often to cover the rather unsightly vegetable bits, and occasionally a bit of high-nitrogen fertilizer to speed up decomposition.

Late the next fall, I dug out a moderate amount of good black stuff from the bottom of the pit, first piling the still-unprocessed stuff off to the side. I filled a wheelbarrow three times with crumbly dark soil that except for here and there bore little resemblance to orange rinds or sprouting potatoes.

I thought this was a pretty decent success, since I knew nature takes its own sweet time to break down a manure pile into usable stuff—two years, maybe more—and I wasn't sure how long it would take a vegetation-only pile to become usable. I was feeling quite smug about my accomplishment when I felt a presence over the fence.

"Competing with the city garbage dump?" asked my neighbour mildly. Normally I appreciated his dry humour, but this time I sensed he was not trying to be amusing. I babbled on about this little pile of detritus being nature in action, about how it was an ancient and honourable practice, about how I was improving the soil while saving space at the garbage dump, but he didn't look convinced.

"It doesn't smell bad, does it?" I asked him, rather plaintively, I fear. I was actually rather proud of its slightly sweet, earthy smell.

"Once in a while I notice it," he replied. I suggested any odour he might detect could be drifting up from the rotting algae on the shores of the lake or the sewage treatment plant, both a mile or so south, but he clearly considered my compost pit the culprit.

I knew he would never have blamed the compost pit for the smell if he hadn't been able to see it. I liked my neighbours, all of them, and I still do, but the time had come for a more substantial fence.

The next spring, around one back corner and halfway up the backyard, we installed a five-foot-high lattice fence that allowed the breezes in, as well as some light. We painted it mouse brown so that it disappeared into the background and felt quite pleased with ourselves because it looked so much more natural than that white picket fence. Twenty-odd years later the fence still stands, added to now so that it extends all the way across the back of the garden and up past the house on one side. It was one of our best garden investments.

We still make compost, too, although the pit disappeared long ago. A few years after the pit experiment the city distributed brown plastic composters, and we acquired two. They worked fine, I suppose, but they couldn't hold all we wanted to put in them, and we'd put out bags of material for recycling on garbage day. A couple of years ago we acquired two four-foot square (and high) joined wooden structures with removable slat sides from a neighbour who was moving, and they're the best. They're big enough to hold almost everything we can feed them, and their volume means they retain heat better and thus the material inside breaks down faster. They look pretty good, too—rustic and natural, as though they might have come from a real farm.

AS EVERYONE WHO reads the science pages of the papers must know by now, two full-grown trees give off enough oxygen over a year to allow a family of four to breathe. Well, there's some confusion over that figure, and maybe it depends on how you figure it—if you can: NASA says that during photosynthesis one full-grown tree produces .67 pounds of oxygen a day, and a full-grown person breathes in 1.85 pounds. That doesn't seem to jibe with the previous figure—it's a bit like comparing apples to oranges. I read somewhere else that in a year an acre of trees provides enough oxygen for eighteen people. The Canadian Forest Service website said that when it comes down to it, trees don't have any significant impact on the oxygen content of the atmosphere. Apparently the seaweed in the earth's oceans give off more of the big O.

No matter. We all agree that trees are invaluable to this Earth because they provide shade and cool the air, in addition to looking good and absorbing gases like carbon monoxide and sulphur dioxide. They've been worshipped by many cultures since ancient times and not because those people had any scientific data to prove their beliefs. A Norse legend, for example, says that the ash tree, the sacred Yggdrasill, begat man. In medieval times trees were thought to heal (a tree with a split trunk was especially valuable because sick persons could pass through it so that they could soak up some of the tree's power), and to endow young women with fertility—this belief is the origin of the maypole dance. In Greek and Roman myths, trees protected spirits: the pine held Pan's; the olive, Athena's. Daphne fled from Apollo and became the laurel. The god Adonis, the Greek god of vegetation, was born of a myrrh tree; the tree was actually his mother, Myrrha, killed and transformed while fleeing her father, who had impregnated her without realizing he'd just had sex with his daughter. . . But that's a tale you'll have to Google for yourself if you want to know more of it. Even in the early years of Christendom, a tree that somehow caused a death, say with a falling branch, could be executed—or cut down and burned—as if it had murderous intent. The tree whose fruit choked to death Drusus, the teenage son of Emperor Claudius, in about AD 25 was summarily destroyed, but I think Drusus's real murderer was actually a jealous relative. We know how bloodthirsty those Romans were.

I can see why trees have had such an influence over man. Even a relatively small one has more presence than a mere human, and large one can be truly imposing, even majestic. Most of them live a long time—some, such as the coast or California redwoods, botanically known as *Sequoia* and native to a narrow strip of northern California and Oregon along the Pacific coast, more than a thousand years. We'd like to be around that long. As the late Christopher Lloyd, one of England's most entertaining writers and best gardeners, wrote in the preface to *The Adventurous Gardener* (1983): "By exercising a little vision [as you get older], you will come to realize that the tree, which has a possible future, perhaps even a great one, may be more important one day than yourself."

I certainly hope that's not going to be true of our Norway maple. I've had a serious competition with that tree, and I'd rather it didn't come out the champ. I lost most rounds in the beginning, as I gradually realized that no matter how much topsoil I laid over its roots in a futile attempt to grow some pretty impatiens or begonias under its branches, those little suckers would always rise to the surface in search of air and sunshine. Years later, when we were doing a house and garden renovation, we dumped yards of subsoil from the excavation and the new beds around the tree and shaped it into a two-foot high berm. Do you think that tree would give in? No way, Jose, as we used to say. Within a year its greedy roots were lurking just under the soil surface again. So I conceded temporary defeat and seeded grass under the tree. It soon became clear that grass wasn't a suitable companion either.

That tree has more serious faults than grasping roots. The canopy is so dense hardly a ray of sunlight can filter through. Its maroon and lime-green flowers, which I admit are rather pretty in a thank-goodness-it's-spring kind of way, produce prolifically, and send thousands of little green keys fluttering all over the garden, lodging in secret corners to germinate and grow where you can't see them till they're stubborn adolescents and won't be dug out. With a few backbreaking hours in spring we control the seedlings in our garden, but many have grown up on our neighbours' properties and now are young adult trees looming over our fence.

I hope I don't sound prejudiced, but this tree doesn't belong here: it's a European immigrant brought to North America more than two centuries ago to grow on our streets precisely because of its adaptability and vigour. I've heard that George Washington himself bought two from a garden supplier for his own estate. Because of its heavy seeding the tree has proliferated and is choking out many of our native species, particularly in Toronto's ravine system. If its numbers and the dense shade don't do in the natives, the toxins the mature Norway maple releases into the soil through its roots will (in similar fashion to the black walnut), by preventing the seeds of other trees from germinating.

This tree is one tough hombre. It's tolerant of compacted soil and a wide range of pH levels; it grows in shade or sun, in extreme heat or in drought. It seems to have no insect enemies.

The Norway maple can be a handsome tree, there's no doubt. I'd say the best-known variety locally is Crimson King, and it's also available with golden yellow leaves (Princeton Gold) and a variegated green-and white leaf (Harlequin). There's a globular variety much shorter than its brothers that seems to be beloved of municipalities and hydro companies because it doesn't grow tall enough to interfere with overhead wiring.

I don't know what alias mine goes by, but it has dark red leaves in spring that fade to green and then become reddish again in fall. The bark is rough and greyish; its limbs are strong and spreading. Visitors sometimes come into our garden and immediately say "What a lovely tree," and then I list its deficiencies. I would never plant this tree, and I wonder why landscape designers still recommend it.

But the tree and I have reached détente. To control its shade we prune it back every couple of years, including some severe limbing-up. Years ago I discovered the tree would permit the close presence of Baltic ivy, winter creeper, and Japanese spurge, so a green mosaic of these three groundcovers hugs its base. And I'm biding my time: the arbourist tells me our tree has a bad case of root girdling, which means its strong root system is gradually wrapping around its base and it will eventually choke itself to death. He's surprised it's lasted as long as it has.

Even if the local bylaws allowed me to do it, I wouldn't cut down a healthy, well-sited tree. I prefer to play the waiting game and let the darn thing do itself in. I already have plans for its replacement: a rustic garden house embraced by a native tree, perhaps a tulip or a coffee tree, plus a few flowering shrubs, a getaway where I can sit and enjoy the view.

DON'T THINK for a minute that while I was indulging my farmer phase and doing battle with a tree I was ignoring flowers. Not on your life. I'd been digging all along, making a rather predictable narrow bed across the back of the house and then a wide island bed running parallel to it, leaving a three-foot strip of grass between. In this ample border I indulged my passion for perennials.

I haunted the nurseries and got myself on the mailing lists of several specialty growers. I bought as many gardening magazines as I could find, but most were directed towards readers in other parts of the world, like England or the U.S., and didn't have much specific growing information that applied to my Canadian garden. (This deficiency, as you'll see, I had a hand in rectifying a few years later at my own magazine.) I tried plants Uncle Ren had never grown, plants that have since become fairly common, such as the daisylike native purple coneflower, with its gorgeous bronzy domelike centres, and feathery pink astilbe that likes a bit of shade (both of which are still dependable kingpins of my garden); obedient plant, which I learned was actually unruly and won't stay in its designated space (I think its common name is misleading—it actually earned it because you can supposedly swivel the individual pink blossoms on its tall stalk up and down; frankly I've never found it particularly agreeable to that move, either); and ligularia The Rocket. Even after I decided I didn't want yellow in my garden anymore I've kept this plant: its golden spikes are cheerful exclamation points in July, and the rich brown seed heads add texture to the landscape in winter.

But perhaps my greatest find during those innocent years was lythrum, commonly known as purple loosestrife. I call these innocent years because although lythrum was a beauty, with tall spires of bright cerise-pink flowers that not only lasted for weeks and brought joy to the garden but also made good cut flowers, it became a national pariah within a few years, condemned for taking over wetlands and choking out plants that wildlife liked to feed on. Garden writers and naturalists demanded that it be taken off the display benches of every nursery in the country. It was another immigrant plant, you see, brought to our country where there were no known insect enemies to keep it in check.

And even though it was hybridized here by Agriculture Canada (at the Morden Research Station in Manitoba) and produced cultivars that were apparently sterile, the species plant was multiplying rapidly and wreaking havoc on our wetlands.

You know, all it takes is one bad species to spoil the whole lot. My lythrum Morden Gleam and Morden Pink had never set seed or spread beyond their designated spaces in my garden, so I stubbornly continued to grow them—stealthily, I admit, never allowing them to appear in a photograph. But then I found a stray seedling, and even though I was certain the seed had blown in from a stand of the species plant growing on a nearby highway embankment, I regretfully dug out all my beloved lythrum and put them out for the city compost pickup. To my mind they were sacrificial plants, dying for a greater environmental cause. I still miss them.

Although Ren never asked for cuttings of the lythrum (maybe he knew something I didn't), on his occasional visits to my garden he often did request cuttings of some of my new plants. I wasn't winning any show prizes for my perfect blooms or arrangements from my garden, but his desire to have some of my plants was red ribbon enough for me. I'd stopped growing his dahlias because they seemed stiff and out of place in my sprawling beds, but we continued our plant exchange. He introduced me to exotica like the dramatic and sophisticated indoor amaryllis and the more common winter aconite, a bright yellow gem that still appears in my garden early every spring, a reminder of my garden mentor.

By this point in its growth my garden was looking pretty good, but I might have known my desired point of attainment was going to elude me again. I was stuck in my old style, growing nice beds of flowers but not making a garden. One day while taking a bag of vegetable peelings down to the compost bins in the back corner of the yard, I had a revelation. I was actually walking along a *path*—one I'd worn in the grass myself by walking from the deck (which Michael, ever money conscious now that he was enrolled in college, had built outside our kitchen door) diagonally across the yard to the compost area. As I turned and walked back towards the house, I realized that the worn grass along the back of the house, between the narrow foundation bed and my wider flower border, was also a path and connected to the first one.

These were pathways I walked frequently while working in the garden. They were perfect examples of form following function and were the beginning of a garden plan that, although altered somewhat, exists to this day as the garden's central design.

CHAPTER 7

Searching

FOR NATURAL STYLE

. . . . .

WHILE TRAVELLING HOME to Mississauga on the commuter train from my job at *Toronto Life* in downtown Toronto, I always made myself stay awake long enough to soak up the view of wildflowers and garden escapees growing with abandon on the railway embankment at the west end of the city. To me it was like an Impressionist painting, a near-blur of colour rushing past the train windows. I realize I was probably romanticizing it—no doubt its beauty had something to do with the speed of the train, which allowed me to ignore the crop of fast-food containers, plastic bags, and bicycle wheels that had been tossed over the fence and took their place among the flowers.

How had the plants got there, I wondered. Had they fled from unhappy gardens? Or had they been discarded, tossed over the fence by ungrateful gardeners who'd tired of them? In their new communal home they flourished, along with the wild-flowers that seeded there naturally, courtesy of the wind and the birds. None of this pretty show was of any value to most of my fellow travellers, who viewed it as a rampant growth of weeds. I'd overhear their comments: "Time they cleaned that garbage up, don't you think?" one would say.

"I bet all those weeds are bothering someone's allergies," his companion would reply.

"They should mow it all down and put in some good grass," another would offer.

I had to agree with them about the garbage, and I wondered why the railway company didn't send a crew to pick up the debris. But to my eyes, tired after a day of editing copy and reading proofs, the view of the embankment was a welcome rest and a reminder that I was going home for a spot of relaxing puttering in my own garden. The railway garden changed from season to season: in spring it was a beautiful range of bright greens mixed with yellows and blues—random clumps of escaped daffodils, stands of dandelions and what looked like bluebells or wild phlox; in summer it could be blue flax and white Queen Anne's lace, rosy milkweed, yellow day lilies and blue or mauve spiderwort; it metamorphosed into glorious goldenrod and black-eyed Susans, mauve asters and white boltonia in fall. And these were only the plants I thought I recognized from the train window— I'm sure many more were hidden among the wild grasses but were contributing subtly to the overall display, like the timpani and triangles in a symphony orchestra. I was always keen to see how the display shifted and altered its colours from week to week.

The embankment faced south and had a steep slope that caught the sun nearly all day. I can't imagine what the soil was like, but if any of the household scraps in the garbage dumped over the fence over the years was able to escape its plastic confines and break down into compost, it was rich indeed. All on its own the garden achieved harmony, balance, and repetition—three favourite words of garden designers and writers—with the wind and birds and Mother Nature as its only assistants. It was obviously biodiverse, with many varieties of plants to attract many different caterpillars and ladybugs, birds, butterflies, and bees, which all competed for survival and maintained the balance of nature. This garden was the kind I wanted—natural, relaxed, full of birds and insects, like a farm meadow.

Alas, that embankment garden disappeared long ago, replaced by stiff plots of boxwood edging and white marble chips replicating the logos of financial institutions and real estate firms. The enterprising person who leases the land from the railway and plants and maintains these "gardens" for the advertisers has tried to give it a natural look with curved plantings of daffodils and shrubs linking the plots along the embankment, but to me these efforts at naturalizing look more like a scalloped pie crust. They're too *deliberate*. I miss the old wild garden—it inspired me, crystallizing my budding interest in meadow gardens and a desire for something nature friendly in my own backyard.

And that is how I fell in with a young man who quite literally led me down the garden path. He was a recent graduate of a horticultural and design program at a local community college, and one of his garden plans had been featured in a story I edited for *Toronto Life*. His plan specified eco-friendly natural beds with a coherent overall design. Just what I wanted. So I called him up.

He was infectiously enthusiastic about the idea of growing a meadow in my backyard, and I immediately bonded with him when he walked with me along the worn grass from the deck to the compost in the back corner and said, "Here's the perfect, natural framework for your meadow—we'll mow it, maybe give it a bit more curve, and it will be the natural pathway though grasses and native plants."

Lovely, I thought, envisioning a miniature field of purple coneflower, native mauve bee balm with its Earl Grey tea fragrance, some spikes of magenta liatris, and wavy blue vervain poking through drifting grasses. Maybe a few daisies and some wands of Culver's root for a touch of white. Perhaps some nodding yellow trout lily and a display of the delicate, starry white foamflower for a billowy display in spring. My mental picture was filled with beauty.

"But do you think a meadow will be too much or too tall for a suburban backyard?" I demurred.

"Don't worry; we'll be sure to use low-growing plants and scatter them near the path, so your neighbours will get used to it."

"So you'll dig out all the grass and replace it with meadow grasses?" I asked.

"Oh, we don't have to take out this grass; we'll just let it grow," he said with a confident air.

"But it's lawn grass," I said. "Will it stand up like meadow grass?"

"Of course," he said. "There's enough fescue in the mixture it to keep it stiff."

I suppose that should have been my first warning, but given that I didn't know much about lawn-grass mixtures I took him at his word. Then he proudly showed me a snapshot of his own downtown garden.

"Look," he said. "Here's my native garden. It's not fully grown yet, but you should be able to get the idea."

88 What I saw was a heavily shaded, narrow gravel laneway wedged between two tall houses with a few sparse plants hugging the brick walls. Two tire ruts ran down the centre of the gravel.

"What's going to happen here is that the grass and plants will grow outward into the lane, around and between the tire ruts. It'll be just like a natural farm laneway," he explained.

"What are the plants?" I asked

"Oh, I've got some Chinese lanterns in there somewhere, a bit of goldenrod, a Virginia creeper, some tansy, some clover. Some things were already there, and I dug some others up out in the country."

It sounded rather vague to me, but I nodded my head, not really understanding whether these qualified as native plants. The Chinese lantern, I knew from experience, is a pretty enough plant with bright orange husks covering inner fruits in fall, but I knew it was native to Europe and southern Asia. It's an adapted wild plant, related to the tomatillo, curiously enough, sometimes sold in nurseries and not technically a weed. But in my garden it had been a conquistador, muscling its way in and taking no prisoners. I'd given some to Matthew for his first garden, and he, too, had found them to be rampant intruders. Doubt was beginning to set in about this young man's qualifications, but he had the degree in garden design, not me.

So he unloaded his mower and cut a wide, curving swath in the grass to outline the newly official pathway. He also cut a circle of grass down near the compost area and the former vegetable garden, which I'd turned into a perennial bed, for a sitting area under our crabapple tree. *Mmm-hmmm.* This was starting to shape up. My confidence was renewed.

"Now," said the young man, turning to our deck. "You should really replace this. It should be bigger. And it's too high; it shouldn't need a railing. A deck shouldn't be level with the back door; you should step *down* a couple of steps from the door to the deck, then one shallow step down to the garden from the deck. D'you see what I mean? That way the deck will be like a low platform connected to the garden, not the house. The transition will be more gradual and graceful."

Yes, I could see what he meant, but his criticism made me feel bad for Michael, who'd built the deck, even though it had come from a lumber company kit and he'd had no control over its design. Moms are like that. I had to agree the deck was too high, however: I felt as though I were sitting on a stage when I was up there, and the three steps down to the garden were narrow and steep. His last suggestion was to use one wide, flat stone for the step from the deck down onto the new mown path, for a natural look. I was sold.

The design elements worked beautifully, and we liked the new circular sitting area in the back corner; I expanded the border of the former-vegetable-now-perennial bed so that it met the curved edge of the mown area. But the meadow was a disaster. Our native plants turned out to be papery cup-shaped Iceland poppies in pink, yellow, and pale orange, big-flowered white shasta daisies, and balloon flower, whose buds look like little pale blue balloons, opening to deeper blue star shapes. None of these grew in any meadow I'd been in. In fact, the shasta daisy looked too much like highly bred cultivars I'd seen in the nursery. Each variety was planted singly at regular intervals so that they were hardly visible in the grass, which grew tall and then fell over in big swirls, like a hundred dogs had been rolling in it. My neighbour started looking over the fence again, this time with pointed offers of his lawn mower.

Chris convinced me we had to do something soon or the neighbours would be calling the bylaw officer. I held on as long as I could, but by midsummer I was digging out the plants so that Chris could cut the grass. There were two hundred plants—I counted every one. They filled out my new perennial bed nicely.

In retrospect, I think I may have known more about plants than this young man, but he was good in the design department. The new deck was far more comfortable and attractive, and the pathway and sitting area gave the garden its shape and form. With a few refinements, these elements still form the backbone of the garden.

EVEN IF I thought I was being innovative with my meadow idea, the truth is that just as in art, architecture, and fashion, garden styles don't develop all by themselves in one person's head. They reflect the social environment of the times. Medieval monks, for example, didn't simply decide they were going to grow only vegetables and medicinal plants and not create showy perennial beds; they were living in the context of their time and followed the rules of a church that preached pleasure in this life meant pain in the next, and pleasure included growing plants solely for their beauty. (Red roses, it was rationalized, represented the blood of Christ and white lilies the Virgin Mary, so both were allowed places in a monastery garden.)

But the beliefs of a dogmatic church were only part of the influences affecting monastery gardens: in the grim earlier days of the Middle Ages, the time after the Visigoths conquered the Roman Empire and its lovely peristyle gardens hidden behind the walls of houses had disappeared, ornamental gardening had become irrelevant. Life was brutal, survival was paramount, and growing vegetables, grains, and medicinal herbs was far more important than raising pretty flowers.

The style of monastery gardens was also culturally influenced. The Persian garden and its four streams of water converging in the centre, which depended on strict geometry for its design, was still a dominant style, and its cruciform plan worked for Christian ideals, too—it symbolized the crucifixion, as well as the points of the compass and the four winds. St. Augustine himself had a role: he was the father of medieval aesthetics and believed the world existed on order, unity, and proportion. "Examine the beauty of bodily form," he wrote in *On Free Choice of Will (De Libero Arbitrio)*, "and you will find everything is in its place by number."

Strict mathematical form in a garden became a microcosm of the perfect design of the universe and dictated such garden forms as the square with a round pool and a pentagonal fountain in the exact centre. Even the wall around the monastery garden had a practical raison d'etre beyond providing privacy for contemplation—it protected inhabitants from the dangers of the forest beyond, which included the pagan gods believed to be lurking in the trees, waiting to claim a poor wayward Christian's soul.

Closer to our time, the Landscape Movement of the late 1700s, led by William Kent and Capability Brown, with its sweeping swaths of grass, curving streams, and copses of trees, was not just England's rejection of continental Europe's formal style of gardening. It was also a reflection of the changes taking place all over England and the continent in agriculture, politics, and science, and the landscape style was further influenced and made acceptable by the new humanist philosophies of the Renaissance. My failed meadow was a child of its own time. It was the '80s, there was a growing movement in North America towards gardens that were friendly to nature and I, as a dedicated nature-loving gardener, was subconsciously responding to it.

But creating flower gardens that reflect nature, both in style and in the practice of gardening, wasn't exactly an idea born in the 1980s. It had its birth in the philosophies of William Robinson, whose book *The Wild Garden* (first published in 1870 and still in print) preached low-maintenance gardens with a natural look and plants that didn't need to be fussed over. This philosophy was opposed to the reigning Victorian idea of intricately planted beds of gaudy annuals that had to be clipped to maintain the pattern and then replaced as they faded, a style Robinson called "the pastry cook's garden"—a description that echoes my own thought about the scallops on the railway embankment. Robinson's more casual garden styles also reflected England's changing social classes: it appealed to hands-on gardeners—the working-class types who couldn't afford hired gardeners, conservatories, and greenhouses as the rich folk could.

Robinson influenced Gertrude Jekyll (she took over from him as editor of England's *The Garden* magazine in 1899) and other garden designers, and his ideas spread to Europe. There, in the early 1900s, they were adapted and taken a step further by people like German garden architect Willy Lange.

Unlike Robinson, who felt that any "exotic" plant (meaning one native to a foreign country, an immigrant plant) should be welcome in a natural garden as long as it was happy in the garden's conditions, Lange insisted on growing only German natives. His ideas fit the political ideals of the National Socialist Party, and by the 1930s the demand in Fascist Germany was for "German plants for German gardens set in German landscapes," as Penelope Hobhouse writes in *The Story of Gardening*. Lange developed the philosophy of a garden perfectly in tune with nature where animals, plants, and gardener held equal rights, and somehow this idea was used politically to discriminate against Jews, who, it was claimed, could not grasp the idea of preserving nature because they were nomadic people.

Horticultural racism had raised its ugly head. Jens Jensen, a Dane who immigrated to the U.S. in 1884 and eventually became an influential garden designer and writer, also rejected foreign plants. He was quite clear about keeping them out of American gardens. "The great destruction brought to our country through foreign importation [will] prove alarming in future," he declared in his 1939 book, *Siftings*. I might agree with him in the case of the Norway maple and a few other unwise and invasive imports, but I think his intent was more sweeping. Like Lange, Jensen felt great contempt for the garden styles of southern Europe, which both men felt were too "architectural."

93

Jensen also condemned the Latin and oriental styles he thought were invading the U.S. and was proud to say that the gardens he created expressed the spirit of America and were free of foreign character.

Still, his dedication to the natural landscape of his chosen country had its good side. Jensen pioneered natural design in North America and paved the way for the use of grasses and native plants in gardens. He loved the prairie light; he truly wanted to preserve North America's native heritage, as well as its wetlands, forests, and grasslands; and he was true to himself: when Henry Ford, for whom he was designing a meadow with native trees underplanted with wildflowers, asked him to fit a formal garden into the design, Jensen quit.

The school of natural gardening sputtered its way through the years after the Second World War and picked up again in the 1970s, influenced by many growers, designers, and writers and by a strong and growing concern for what civilization is doing to our environment. In today's world the natural movement has a lot of influence on plant choices as well as on garden design, and it means at the least that gardeners have adopted the idea of using plants that will happily grow without undue efforts to keep them alive. In other words, most know enough not to try to grow woodland plants in a dry, sunny backyard, or sun-loving meadow plants in a forested lot. They're also discovering that gardening is a lot easier this way.

At the more dedicated end of the natural gardening movement are landscape architects and designers who plan prairies and meadows for public parks and municipal centres—gorgeous, controlled sweeps of grasses and native plants that take your breath away—and serious garden-variety gardeners like the writer-photographer I know who has a planted meadow at the entrance to her ten-acre country property. I covet it, but I realize now that my comparably small suburban property is simply not the place for a meadow. I can practise gardening in tune with nature and follow a style that pleases me and has a loose, natural look but still fits into my neighbourhood's more conformist style, without having to plant a meadow or a wild garden.

Especially an untended one. I've seen some pretty wild and messy gardens in urban areas, and although I empathize with the gardeners' intentions, I wonder if they might consider the context of their gardens. Perhaps those lovers of natural gardens who claim a high moral purpose and let their gardens grow rampantly and without care might stop to think that a wild garden needs some taming in the city—and my criticism is by no means a support of neighbours who complain or city parks departments who come in and cut gardens down when the owner is away. I've read about them. I think it's a serious step backward to reject gardens that look different simply because they don't live up to rigid neighbourhood standards of clipped grass and foundation plantings. But gardeners who prefer a more natural and eco-friendly style also have to have respect for their communities. A natural garden shouldn't be one that's left to grow on its own; it requires trimming, weeding, and care, just like any garden.

All these things, and more, I've learned from reading about gardeners and gardening in books and newspaper and magazine articles from ancient to contemporary times. What I've read has entertained and informed me as much as anything I've read, but it seems to me that very little garden writing is truly appreciated. It almost never makes it to the bestseller lists or—except perhaps for Pliny the Elder's *Natural History* (*Naturalis Historia*)— achieves anthropological status as a record of how people live. Perhaps people will always look upon gardening as a hobby without much importance, as something women or older people do, but I've come to realize it's an important social necessity. For me, it used to be something I did that made me feel better, but then it developed into *what I did*. In many ways it defines me.

The other thing I've learned from reading about gardening is that we probably do almost nothing in our lives, even making a garden, without influence from sources of which we're unaware.

THE YOUNG meadow man entered my life again unexpectedly a few years later.

We had decided our front entrance needed sprucing up, if not a whole new facelift. The original off-the-shelf concrete pathway pavers and moulded concrete steps leading to the front door not only looked narrow and inhospitable, but they were also beginning to crumble. We needed a better entryway plan and someone to implement it, so I called a big local nursery with a design department and asked if they could send someone over.

A familiar cheery face called hello as the truck pulled into our driveway. "Hey, I got a new job with this here fancy outfit, and I'm so happy you called them. I'm dying to see the meadow!" he said as he jumped out onto the driveway. "How's it going?"

"Um . . . well . . . ah . . . the neighbours didn't like it," I stammered. "I'm afraid we had to take it out . . ."

Why was I being such a wimp? Why didn't I tell him I'd had a problem with it myself?

. "You didn't *cave!*" the young man said, looking shocked. "You took it out? But you were so happy with it."

96

In one of those tell-all conversations mothers and daughters sometimes indulge in, Suzy once told me I sometimes misled people on my real feelings—she didn't exactly use the word hypocritical, but I'd wondered. Maybe from my first doubt about the meadow I should have been more forthright with this young man.

"I'm afraid it had to go," I said, squaring my shoulders and deepening my voice. "The grass flopped over because it wasn't the right kind. You'd said it would be okay, but it wasn't."

"It would have been okay if you'd given it more time to find its natural growth habit," he countered. Never say die, I thought. Well, I knew his strengths and weaknesses and was determined to dismiss him summarily if he headed in the wrong direction this time. I told him what we were thinking and he came through just as before: enthusiastic and full of ideas, some of them half-baked.

He dashed about, taking measurements and making sketches on a big pad. He studied the existing foundation plantings, looking under their leaves and examining their underpinnings; he checked under the front stoop and paced out a path around to the back of the house. He looked very professional.

"I have some splendid ideas for you," he finally said, exuding the old confidence. "Let's sit here on the steps and go over them."

The design he proposed was, as before, exactly what I was looking for, even if I hadn't known it till he showed me his sketch. He proposed a full makeover: removing the concrete-slab path and putting in a much wider one of flagstones set in pea gravel that would curve from the driveway to the front steps. Five wide steps, not four, up to the front stoop, lower in the rise and deeper for the foot, so that the ascent to the front door would be more gradual and safer.

"The new steps and the wider and slightly curving path will make the approach to your front door more hospitable," he said. I agreed totally.

"Then, we want a deeper and wider front stoop, as wide as the new steps, and everything in stone to match the pathway flagstone," he said.

Of course.

"Now, here's my excellent idea," he said with a big grin. "We take this path all the way around to the back, and all across the back of the house—in pea gravel only in the back, no flagstone, to cut some cost—and join it up with the other path in the back garden. We'll gravel the whole thing."

Yes, yes, I nodded vigorously.

"And now, my *most* excellent idea!" He was nearly jumping up and down. "Right here at the front, just as the path curves to go around the side of the house, we'll bulge it out into a wide semicircle to hold a table and chairs, or a lounger or whatever, so that you can sit out for after-dinner coffee and watch your neighbours go by!"

"Yes, yes, *yes!*" I shouted. I was nearly jumping up and down myself. It was indeed a good idea, and I wished I'd thought of it.

I liked his idea for the foundation beds, too—to take out what remained of the grass in front of the foundation plantings and pull the beds right out to the pathway, to raise the earth to the level of the front stoop and slope it down to the path, and to fill the beds with interesting plants.

I stopped feeling so enthusiastic at the interesting plants part.

"Here," he said, pointing to a spot about five feet from the dining room window, "we'll put in a black walnut. It has lovely bark you'll appreciate as you go up the pathway, and a really nice leaf pattern."

"A black walnut?" I said incredulously. "But they grow at least forty feet tall!"

"That's okay; you can bonsai it." He started to tell me how I could do that, by cutting back the roots and the limbs a couple of times a summer, and maybe wiring the stems for shape, but he'd lost me. I knew it would never work and we'd be pulling out that tree a year or two after we'd put it in. I tuned out his other suggestions, but I remember they included a stand of bamboo and a Japanese-style stone basin with a bamboo spout dribbling water near the corner of the house (where there was no electricity to power a submersible pump) and a big bed of cactus under the front window. I didn't believe his protestations that cactus was hardy in my part of Ontario, but it is, actually—I know that now because now I have two, one exactly in the spot he recommended.

I told him how much I liked his design and said we would do the work and the planting, if he could just provide us with some kind of to-scale plan . . .?

I felt I was being assertive and truthful enough. He happily agreed, sorry to lose the construction and planting business for his new employer but encouraged by my compliments about his design. He climbed back in his truck with a promise to deliver the plans within a week.

As he drove off, I realized I'd forgotten to ask him about his alleyway garden.

❦

CHAPTER 8

A Hobby
BECOMES A JOB

. . . . .

URNING ONE'S HOBBY into a job might have negative con-
notations to people who look upon it as turning something
pleasurable into hard work. But finding a job where you can
follow your favourite hobby all day long—now that's a positive.
And this was my lucky situation after I took the job as editor of
the brand new *Canadian Gardening* magazine at the beginning
of a brand new decade, 1990; I stayed there for nine years, the
longest I'd spent at any magazine.

People who work on Canadian magazines are a peripatetic lot,
moving frequently from one publication to another as they gain
experience and hone their skills. I was no different from other
editors in this regard, spending a handful of years at *Weekend*,
five more at the city magazine *Toronto Life*, a year at *Chatelaine*,
and a couple at another women's magazine, *City Woman*, thence
to a lifestyle magazine, and so on. In there somewhere was a
stint on the public affairs staff of the Toronto Transit Commis-
sion, handling its employee publication and the annual report,

among other jobs. I was managing editor of *Vista*, a relatively short-lived business magazine the whole staff knew was about to turn its navel upside when one day the editor-in-chief came into my office.

"I just got a call from a headhunter who's looking for an editor to head up a new gardening magazine," she said; she'd been to my house a few times and teased me about being a closet gardener. "You're a natural for the job, and given the situation around here the timing is perfect. Can I pass on your name?"

Yes, indeed she could. The day after I accepted the job, before I'd even had a chance to tell the editor-in-chief that I would be leaving, the axe fell at *Vista*. My stars were still aligned.

And thus began my further education as a gardener.

CANADIAN GARDENING started to publish in 1990, just as gardening was being embraced by fortysomething boomers as the hobby of the month—or decade, as it turned out. Although a few regional Canadian gardening magazines existed, *Canadian Gardening* was the first to cover our country from sea to sea, and it did so with glossy paper and colour on every page. This kind of production is not cheap, even if it does seem like an obvious requirement for a gardening magazine, so it was a big step for the small company that finally decided to hire me to be in charge of their new magazine. The magazine was the dreamchild of the company's editorial director at the time—as a gardener of roughly boomer age himself he had a gut feeling that gardening was going to blossom into a strong trend, and he was right. Gardening was about to take off as the next obsession embraced by his peers.

We started with a tiny staff: me and Beckie Fox, a part-time copy editor and fact checker who became our full-time assistant editor after a year, then became managing editor, and took

over as editor after I left at the end of 1998. I leaned on Beckie
a lot over the years. And we had the cheery and capable Gloria
Wilkinson, a shared secretary/typist/general dogsbody (shared
because the company also published a handful of other hobby
magazines) whom we couldn't have done without. When I look
back on those early issues I see much room for improvement and
a lot to be proud of, but I'm also left wondering how our magazine ever made it into mailboxes and onto newsstands, given the
paucity of our staff.

In our roughly eighty pages (the magazine and its staff have
grown since those early days, just like my Norway maple) we
covered as much as we could that a gardener might want to
know—garden profiles and makeovers, growing and mainte-
nance, garden projects and design, stories on the environment,
indoor plants, water gardens... Regular columnists covered
specific topics, and at the publisher's request we had recipes—
but at our editorial insistence only for homegrown garden
produce. One year we ran a series on how to design and plant
colour-themed gardens (pink was popular, but Sissinghurst
white was *hot*) and we did stories on wild urban gardens, native
plants, plant names, and rock gardens. The topics reflected our
own interests, for sure—Beckie was also a serious gardener, on
her way to becoming a Master Gardener, and Gloria grew roses
to die for (she's English, of course) and wintered over her gera-
niums in her garage, something I have never dared to try. But
we felt we were a microcosm of gardeners in general, and what
we liked they'd like. I like to think we were generally on target.

We didn't strive to be a coffee table magazine, though we
envied the gorgeous photography and larger page sizes in more
expensive English and American magazines, which we drooled
over while knowing many of the plants pictured would never
survive in our cold-climate gardens and we would never own

a century-old stone wall on which to grow roses. No, we were
a magazine for Canadians who coped with early fall frosts and
January thaws, gardeners who dug and planted and weeded—
and usually designed—their own gardens. We didn't go to landscape architects or designers looking for large or extravagant
gardens to feature; we went to real gardeners. And gardeners
responded: circulation kept rising in increments of a few thousand at every new subscription report. They liked us—they
really liked us!

Well, sometimes they disagreed with us. For a small magazine, we got a lot of letters—our readers didn't stint on feedback,
both negative and positive. I remember the man who wrote after
our story about pink-themed gardens appeared. He complained
that pink was wimpy and feminine, that we were encouraging
trendiness with this series, and that we should hire more male
writers to give our magazine some substance. In the firm conviction that all sides deserve their view we printed his letter and
received a tart response from a reader who told us in no uncertain terms that if we wasted any more space on letters from sex-
ists like him she'd be cancelling her subscription.

A woman wrote to wonder where on Earth we found "those
awful gardens" we featured on our pages. That stung, but I
wondered what garden-design utopia she lived in. In contrast,
another wrote with compliments for the "real gardens made by
real people," and another for a "practical, honest, and readable
magazine." Some revealed their gardeners' concerns for the environment by complaining about the plastic wrapper holding extra
advertising that the magazine was sometimes mailed in: "Even
if you consider it biodegradable, it's not satisfactory. In a landfill,
nothing is truly biodegradable," wrote one. Others requested or
offered seeds or tidbits of information. "The flower on the Quebec flag is not an iris but the Madonna lily, and many of us are

working to replace it with *Iris versicolor*," wrote a gardener from that province. I was beginning to feel that I knew these people.

A man who obviously liked to delve into the arcane details of language told us the "n" in *officinalis*, as in *Calendula officinalis*, a pretty orange or bright yellow multipetalled marigold popular with medieval monks, didn't simply mean it held official status as a monk-grown plant—it indicated it was approved for medical uses and that the word "officinal" still exists in modern English. Well, I hadn't known that; I looked in my dictionary, and there it was—"Officinal *adj.* 1. Prepared and kept in stock, as drug preparations."

A man from New Brunswick threw us a challenge. Just after our second issue was released he wrote to say he was giving us a year to offer him good, solid information about gardening in his part of the world. "I beg you not to bore us cool-zone gardeners with a constant bombardment of articles about Canada's banana belt," he wrote, meaning southwestern Ontario and southern British Columbia. He promised to renew only if we lived up to his expectations. He was true to his word—a year later he sent us a cheque for another couple of years' subscription. "You succeeded. Keep it up," he wrote.

As someone with western roots I understood his point. We could never be Toronto-centric. People outside the city, especially those outside the Toronto/Niagara megalopolis, abhor any hint of narcissism from this most populated part of the country, whether it has to do with gardening or politics or the arts. From the beginning I was resolved to include in every issue major stories from the east and the Prairies, as well as from northern regions, and to go light on the "banana belt." Nevertheless, if we didn't separate stories about Ontario and the West Coast by at least a couple of issues, we'd get banana-belt complaint letters.

I finally started keeping a log of how many stories we'd run from each region, and I'd reply as politely as I could that we were striving to include the whole country and the score was now thirty-five to five in favour of the Prairies and the east coast, or whatever the numbers were at the particular time. After about five years, the ad director innocently enquired one day whether we had anything against southern Ontario gardens—we had included so few—and I realized that perhaps I was in danger of overcompensating.

Finding photogenic gardens and relevant horticultural topics in a country as dispersed and diverse as Canada takes some doing. I may have lived in three cities and one small rural village in my lifetime, and visited both the Maritimes and the West Coast, but I couldn't say I was fully informed about its gardens, and by my second year as editor realized that I had to do some travelling. This task was pleasant, although tiring. Each spring and summer I'd make two or three scouting trips to cities and towns in the east and the Prairies, or to northern Ontario and the West Coast, and to driving-distance locations in Quebec and Ontario. Usually I'd cold-call the local horticultural society ahead of my visit and ask to be pointed in the direction of a few good gardens to look at, and almost without exception I'd be offered more than a list of places to see—I'd be provided with a car and driver as well. (Of course, the magazine covered their expenses, unless they wanted to be good hosts and simply wouldn't accept any compensation.)

All the people I met were inspiring and helpful, but in Calgary they were overachievers: they met me at the airport with a van and four escorts, showed me ten gardens a day for three days (to be honest, it was all a blur each day after number five; it's a good thing I took scouting shots and kept a notebook), and feted me with a barbecue and a special lunch. Their gardens surprised and amazed me. They were lush and fulsome, filled with colour and bristling with healthy plants, the beds set against a gorgeous deep blue prairie sky.

Having lived on the Prairies I knew its summers are mostly like that—hot, dry, and full of strong colour, with that glowing sky sitting like a dome overhead. It was the chill Calgary evenings I wasn't prepared for—"It'll be late July when you're here; better bring a down jacket if you have one," said my cold-call contact on the phone. I came to love the backyard firepits that allowed garden viewing after 7 PM and warmed your toes at an outdoor barbecue. I also heard the gardeners' horror stories about the chinooks, which, like most Canadians, I'd always envied. Imagine a warm wind bouncing capriciously over the Rockies and down the foothills on a bleak winter day and turning the weather into spring for an hour or an afternoon!

Chinooks may be welcomed by those suffering from a case of SAD, but not by gardeners. A chinook can melt away the protective blanket of snow and fool plants into yawning and stretching and thinking about a young bud's fancy. Then the warm wind dances away, Jack Frost returns, and there goes the garden.

All the places I travelled to were welcoming and unique—the warm, down-to-earth Newfoundlanders with their Irish-lite accents and tiny gardens in front of the brightly painted houses stepping up the hilly streets in St. John's; the West Coasters, proud of their casual lifestyle (where being "laid back" seems to be a badge of honour) and English-style gardens, but seemingly oblivious to the handsome, dense hedges that are a hallmark of Vancouver, as far as I can tell. I expected to see lovely gardens, but I was impressed with the hedges, especially the tall, lustrous ones of English and Portuguese laurel—the former with yellow green leaves and the latter with dark green ones—so beautifully clipped in architectural shapes. Neither have I seen cedar or yew hedges so beautiful anywhere else in Canada, as thick, green, and beautifully shaped as they are in England. Of course, the southern part of the West Coast has the advantage of milder winters and longer growing seasons than the rest of us, even where I live in southern Ontario.

Northern Ontario from Sudbury to Thunder Bay was a juxtaposition of the tame and the rugged in both gardens and landscapes—I think of the serene Japanese garden with a traditional tea house and an arched wooden bridge over a gardener-made stream, hidden behind a plain Thunder Bay bungalow, and the large country property with a glorious garden of native plants on a natural rock formation high over a narrow, rushing river.

The variety and grandeur of our natural landscapes really impressed me. I couldn't get my fill of the rugged forests on Nova Scotia's southeast coast and through northern Ontario, and the mountain wildflower meadows near Banff. More unusual was the meadow south of Sudbury, where I didn't know wildflower meadows existed; it was a huge outdoor oriental carpet of yellow and orange hawkweed, fragrant bedstraw, and red sheep sorrel. There were more entrancing colours to soak up: the foaming whitecaps, dark blue ocean, and red ochre soil along the coast of Prince Edward Island; and the blue, yellow, and deep green patchwork quilt of flax, canola, and grains I could see from a Dash 8 over the Prairies, its squares stitched together by long, solitary highways and embellished by the occasional farm and silo. I'd seen a similar view years earlier over France, with tiny villages, church steeples, and stone fences providing the stitching, and had thought it was a subject for an Impressionist painting. Here was the pattern in my own country—with more generous squares, as befits a much larger country. And if you think the view from the air is the only way to appreciate the beauty of the Prairies, you haven't stood in a small Saskatchewan village at sunset or sunrise and looked towards the horizon. The layers of brown, green, tan, and yellow, topped with striations of shimmering gold, purple, pink, peach, and turquoise, will drown your soul.

My travelling yielded contacts with some great gardeners and garden groups across the country and stuffed our files with stories to feature in the magazine over the following year or so, but it did much more than that. It taught me about my own country. You can learn a lot from a distance by reading, watching, and listening, but in a country like Canada, spread out in a thin layer over thousands of miles of disparate conditions and diverse populations, nothing compares with seeing things for yourself. My travels for the magazine informed me about my country and turned me into something of a patriot, and I believe that if we were all able to travel its length and breadth at a relatively young age, we would understand each other a lot better.

WITHIN A COUPLE of years *Canadian Gardening* had developed cachet. Radio stations and newspapers called for our sage comments on such imperatives as what were the latest trends in gardening, why gardening had become so popular, and what was the right thing to wear while working in the garden. A lot of these questions seemed pointless to me at the time and still do, but I tried to answer them as thoughtfully and sincerely as I could with, of course, a catchy quip for radio or television (they sometimes called, too)—media that like a nice fifteen-second clip to capture the point. No long-winded answers, please.

On occasion the gods in charge of grey matter were with me. I remember a radio interviewer asking me what was the most difficult place in Canada to garden, likely expecting me to say Whitehorse, Yukon, or Churchill, Manitoba, but after a split-second of panic I said "Calgary" with calm conviction, taking myself by surprise. What part of my brain had dredged up that bit of information?

"Really. Why?" asked the interviewer, intrigued. As I recall she was from Winnipeg, not exactly the mildest climate in Canada.

"Well, because of the chinooks," I replied, realizing it was indeed a legitimate opinion on a topic I'd briefly discussed around a firepit with a handful of fellow gardeners. Sometimes your subconscious works harder than you think. I went on to explain how good and fine chinooks were for ordinary people paralyzed by winter, and how hard they were on gardens. As I recall, it was one of my finest moments.

I scored another success with the question "What should a new gardener wear in the garden?" I was asked this in the early '90s, when expensive garden smocks and hats, and pants with pockets and loops for holding the secateurs and trowel, were being sold by shops eager to cash in on the gardening craze. But the so-called grunge look of droopy old clothes and layered T-shirts was *de rigueur* among the younger set (seems to me it still is), and that was my spontaneous answer. The grunge look, of course! Good heavens, why would anyone mucking about in the earth wear an appliquéd smock? In summer I wear now, as I did then, my old gym shorts; for goosebump weather I don my husband's discarded summer pants with big pockets and belt loops. His old kneepads from his early touch football days used to come in handy for my hurting knees, but now that I've had knee replacement surgery I sit on a plastic bench. To hold the necessary tools, I carry a six-quart fruit basket painted red. And what are stained and torn T-shirts for but weeding or digging in the garden? Goodwill wouldn't dream of taking them, and I believe in reusing and recycling.

I had more trouble coming up with a definitive answer to the frequent question about why gardening had suddenly become the hobby of the decade. Try to answer that and sound authoritative when you have no statistics to support your points, just seat-of-the pants observations!

I decided to trust my posterior. I first trotted out some accepted wisdom: "Well, we can blame those powerful baby boomers again . . . they're a significant influence. After all, when the largest chunk of the population likes something, it becomes a trend. Then the horticultural industry responds, bringing more plants and new hybrids to the market, and the ball is rolling."

It was harder to answer the natural follow-up question: Well then, why did the baby boomers embrace gardening as their hobby, instead of, say, lawn bowling? I'd been around a bit and I'd observed my younger neighbours, and I had a simple theory about this issue. Because most of them had married later than the generation before them and put off babies and home owner-ship till their late thirties, they were now settling down. Home improvements, including having a garden for the kids and dogs and alfresco dinner parties, was where they were going to spend their money. And as with all new gardeners (I'd done it myself), the boomers were reinventing the gardening wheel. They were discovering basic practices such as composting (one woman asked me if there was a recipe, and did she need an activator to get it going or a thermometer to know when it was done?), and feeling the same impatience for a perfect garden that I once had. They wanted the newest plants, unique varieties no one had seen before. They wanted white gardens like the one at Sissing-hurst. They wanted a "garden of rooms," which garden writers in magazines like mine were presenting as the latest style con-cept. Some of my neighbours even wanted my garden, a fact that flattered me immensely, and they'd stop by as they walked the dogs and the kids after supper and ask how I'd come up with the planting plan for the spring bulbs or what was the name of that plant over there and where could they get it. I knew in my bones they were keen to garden because everyone said it was the thing to do, and that was my considered answer.

I left the magazine nearly ten years ago, and I'm still being asked about the latest trends. What's this year's colour combination? Is water gardening still in? Are ornamental grasses the way to go this season?

What is this preoccupation with trends? Gardening isn't fashion; trends don't come and go from year to year in the gardening world, because they can't—it takes at least three seasons to bring a new perennial border to full, satisfying bloom, or to establish that bed of ornamental grasses. And once you've put in a pond and waterfall you're not going to take it out any time soon.

Admittedly, you can plant a hot garden of the latest orange, purple, and yellow annuals for that fashionable "colour hit" and toss the plants out when fall frost kills them dead, but when it comes to real gardens, nature takes its own sweet time. Styles evolve, too, and they're often based on practical use. I like to use the "garden of rooms" example: considered a brilliant new concept by many in the mid-'90s, it's actually been a strong influence in garden design since the time of the Romans, and the recovered gardens at Pompeii and Herculaneum prove it. Medieval monks had garden "rooms" for different purposes: herbers for medicinal plants and kitchen gardens for fresh vegetables; cloisters for contemplation and infirmary gardens for the convalescent. The Renaissance Italians divided their vast estates geometrically, with grottoes, vistas and views, secret gardens, gardens of hedges and statuary, and complicated water gardens with rills, jets, and cascades of water, all united with the villa by means of connecting terraces, steps, and pergolas. The French aristocracy before the revolution designed extravagant garden parterres for roses or herbs, or simply for postprandial strolling. Vita Sackville-West and her husband, Harold Nicolson, used yew, boxwood hedges, and pleached limes, plus some of the original walls on the grounds of Sissinghurst, to create discrete enclosures, including the famous white garden, a cottage garden, and a rose garden. Thomas Church, perhaps the most influential North American garden designer of the mid-twentieth century, said that gardens are for people—in fact, he wrote a book with exactly that title in the '50s—and should have areas of use for various activities; his ideas influenced my first garden, as well as my present one.

So you see, we didn't invent the garden of rooms; we just rediscovered it—again.

MEANWHILE, back at the ranch, a new garden was under way. I suppose you could say the backhoe made me do it.

We had renovated our little house and added to the kitchen at the back and the living room at the side, and this had required the services of a backhoe. The backhoe was instrumental in my planting-in-mass epiphany: before it could destroy the garden in the fall, I'd removed the island border across the back of the house and stuffed the plants in groups of the same variety (so that I would be able to locate them easily in spring) into what I thought would be a temporary plot on the other side of the pathway. In the spring the planting looked better than the old garden ever had, with the early plants blooming their heads off in masses of colour, and I decided to make this temporary bed permanent.

But the rest of the garden was looking tatty and ordinary to my jaded, well-travelled eyes, and I rationalized that it was incumbent on me, as the editor of a gardening magazine, to have a well-designed, well-tended garden. Who knew who might drop in? First I streamlined my colour scheme, getting rid of some of the yellow flowers and all the orange ones, even the beautiful butterfly weed, a cousin of the common roadside milkweed, which blooms in eye-stopping colour and attracts butterflies. I rather regretted turfing out this plant, but I definitely wanted to rid the garden of the orange tiger lilies I'd bought one year and that kept multiplying. I dug up all I could see and delivered them to Matthew and Suzy, who had both married and had new gardens. Funny, I've never seen my lilies growing in their gardens—maybe they don't like orange either—but they keep reappearing in the most unexpected places in mine. Guess they're here to stay.

I also hired a landscape architect I'd become acquainted with, a local fellow whose own garden I admired immensely and which had appeared in our magazine, and he did a redesign. Well, he didn't so much redesign the garden as refine it, and he pulled it together perfectly. He drew up a plan based on circles and squares (he called it "curvilinear flow") and designed a huge new bed based on two side-by-side circles; the bed extends from a square gravelled sitting area outside the new French doors at the back of the house down to the circular sitting area at the back and out to the lattice fence on the side. "You need more planting space," said he, who apparently knew me better than I thought he did. This meant taking out all the grass in that side of the yard, but I was happy to see it go. A stepping-stone path with a central birdbath meanders through this large garden to allow access to the plants and a pleasant stroll through the flowers.

The main gravel pathway, the spine of the garden that dates back to before its mown meadow birth, was reshaped to curve around the circles that give this bed its shape. It curves slightly out of view in a couple of places, hinting at what's beyond.

My friend also enlarged the side deck redesigned by my meadow man so that it would extend past the kitchen addition and allow a view of the garden; into the deck he inset a small square pond and added a Japanese-influenced arbour overhead as protection from the noon sun. The Japanese motif was repeated in another arbour and low fence at the back of the garden that cunningly hides the compost area. The arbour was an inspiration: the two brown plastic composters at the back of the garden had been a bit of an eyesore, but once the French doors were installed in the living room, a renovation priority so that we could get a good view of the garden from indoors, they loomed like squat ogres on the property line and were the first things I saw when I looked out with my coffee and newspaper in the morning.

I'd read about a man in New York who had a proper formal garden designed like a wheel behind his expensive brownstone, and dead in the centre, instead of a statue or a fountain or sundial, and performing as a focal point as seen from his house windows, sat a large, steaming compost pile. But he was a well-known environmentalist, and maybe he felt he had to keep up appearances. I had no such compunctions; style was as important to me as being in tune with nature. The new fence and arbour, now covered with greenery, made my compost bins disappear.

I can't blame the backhoe for the front garden, which followed about 1995, a few short years after the redesign of the back. My friend had been right—I did need more space for plants. But there were other reasons to take over the front lawn: it was a green and pleasant enough place, but it was barren—no bees, birds, and butterflies to populate it, no colour or scent. The back was nature friendly, and I had learned the value of biodiversity. I'd become an eco-convert. I wanted to make a statement as well as have more space for a garden that would attract nature.

I succeeded, too, although it took me a few years. I had to convince Chris that he wanted to get rid of the grass, and I had to woo my neighbours, all of whom apparently believed in the superiority of the North American lawn. My front garden grew gradually, from a wide border along the driveway and the front path that Chris initially agreed to, and eventually to the full monty, courtesy of an attack of white grubs. One year a big infestation ate the rest of the grass, and to get rid of them a lawn-care guy told us we'd have to use diazinon and kill all the bugs within its reach, including good ones like earthworms. Chris didn't like this idea and reluctantly agreed to let the rest of his lawn become garden. Together we made a narrow gravel pathway to wind through it, and over the next year I jammed the new garden with shrubs, roses, perennials, ground covers, and spring bulbs; soon it was also filled with the hoped-for bees, birds, and butterflies, and a few neighbourhood cats. In the process the front garden became the subject for many talks to horticultural societies and, ultimately, a book.

It's also influenced the neighbours, who at first looked askance at the process but soon decided it was an asset to the neighbourhood. Those who thought differently had the good sense to avoid the subject, suspecting, I presume, they would be in for a sermon on biodiversity from me. It makes me warm all over to see now, a decade later, the march of front-yard gardens of many types down my street. Not all are as packed with plants nor as extensive as mine—many are wide borders or large island beds, with lawn making up about half of the front yard—but our street has moved away from typical foundation plantings and conforming wall-to-wall green lawns. One garden has a southwestern look, with many drought-resistant plants like mullein and yucca and a dry riverbed of stones and gravel; another is all hostas and ferns growing beneath a large tree, with a small sitting area at the bottom of the front steps. All the new front yards are different and reflect their owners' tastes, but, best of all, they're the beginning of a network of gardens that will bring our community more in tune with nature.

CHAPTER 9

Gardening
PARTNERS

. . . . .

SINCE CHRIS WAS instrumental in the making of the front garden, I think the time has come to tell you more about him and his introduction to the world of gardening.

Just after I'd become editor of *Canadian Gardening* magazine, Chris confessed that in our early years together, after we'd bought our little house and I was busily growing vegetables and experimenting with the meadow garden, he'd rush about on Saturday mornings doing his "yard chores" just as he'd done as a teenager so that he could get away to play football or baseball, whatever was on the calendar that day.

Did he think I hadn't noticed? With a trowel or something in my hand I'd watch him drive away excitedly to meet his buddies, only too happy to leave my expectations of him behind. I must say I wondered what the future held for us.

These were the points I'd mull over as Chris drove off, and I assumed he did the same, although not likely as he was anticipating his next touchdown.

It wasn't that he didn't appreciate how the garden enhanced our landscape or that he didn't relish the taste of the fresh greens and tart-sweet tomatoes I was growing. It wasn't that he didn't appreciate what gardening meant to me—I'd certainly told him how important its therapeutic benefits were, if they weren't already obvious to him. He simply had no instinct for gardening and cared little about how things grew, while I could lose an afternoon deadheading or weeding or watching an ant carry a crumb twice its size back to its nest. Being in the garden for me is like being in church for religious folk.

Gardening was my avocation; football and baseball were his. In the early years I worried about other differences, too—he didn't like ballet or symphony concerts, or going to art galleries or plays. I was older—still am, as a matter of fact, although the age difference seems to have shrunk over the years. I had children and he didn't, and wouldn't, if he stayed with me. But we had many things in common beyond a basic sharing of values and an attraction to each other: we loved travelling to distant countries and going to movies together and dissecting them afterward; we were both editors and writers and shared an interest in language, even if it sometimes was reduced to reading aloud to each other the errors in syntax we'd found in that morning's newspaper. He liked to cook, too, although he wasn't as accomplished as I was in the kitchen. And we can't forget his delicious sense of humour. Best of all, we liked and respected each other.

In the long haul, my early concerns were unfounded, although how we resolved our differences remains a mystery to both of us. Today, three decades after we met, we have a lot more common ground—alas, not including ballet and symphony concerts, but I go with a friend. And Chris has come to take pleasure working in the garden, although it's still my bailiwick. Like many couples I came to know through my work, and

like many celebrity gardeners I've read about, we share duties—
he's the brawn and I'm the brains. Well, he does the heavy work
and I provide the artistic input, with some exceptions.

How did this happy situation come about after we moved
back to Mississauga and I became a vegetable fanatic and then
an obsessed flower gardener? I like to think it was because of
my superior powers of persuasion, but down deep I know it had
more to do with my realization that I was expecting too much. I
wanted Chris to share my interests, but he never expected me to
join him at the fifty-five-yard line or even to root for his team
from the bench. I wanted him to feel as I did about gardening,
to take part in it with me, even though some of its appeal for me
is its solitary, even meditative, qualities. But he never expected
me to adopt his interests, and in fact he fulfilled his obliga-
tions before he left to follow his own pursuits. For some reason
I got smart—I took a hands-off approach, a technique akin to
attracting more flies with honey than vinegar, a little lesson my
grandma taught me. There's nothing worse than a nag.

But perhaps I'm taking too much credit for insight. We
talked about this once, and Chris said his interest in gardening
grew because he grew. He decided he liked to work around the
house, and he could see that the garden, and maybe even gardening itself, had its benefits. Football was more fun, but gardening had its place.

Our garden rapprochement began right after we were married in 1983. The fact that we got married in the first place is, to
me anyway, proof that I had some powers of persuasion, since
Chris thought marriage would be an unnecessary development
in an already fine relationship. But a few years after we moved
into our house I proposed—and I prevailed, appealing to his
sense of logic: Well, we owned a house together, didn't we? We
were devoted to each other, weren't we? We expected to stay
together, right? So, why not?

He said yes. It turned out his main objection to getting married was the wedding—marching down a church aisle and hosting a crowded, expensive reception were not on his list things to do. Neither were they on mine. We had a small family ceremony, with Suzy as my witness and Chris's younger brother as his, and the reception for eighty friends and relatives was in our garden on the hottest day of the year, with catered finger food and lots of wine. It was a lovely afternoon. In the snapshots we look like a couple of lovesick teenagers gazing into each other's eyes.

A year or so later we compared notes on the progress of our union.

"Since we got married, you're less possessive," he said. "You allow me to do what I want to do."

"And you are more responsive," I said. "You seem more aware of how I feel. I think you love me more than you used to."

"Well, that could be," he replied after a moment. And then, with that familiar deadpan look I get when a discussion is veering into muddy waters: "Could this mean I love you more than you love me?"

He'd made me laugh again, and that ended the talk. Psychologists can make what they will of our discussion, but the wedding was a turning point, in the garden and elsewhere.

"THIS JUNIPER is an overgrown mess," said Chris the summer after we were married. "We need to do something about it."

He was right, although I hadn't looked at it closely up until then. The juniper in question, close to the property line between ours and the neighbours' backyard, must have been nearly thirty years old at the time. It provided privacy, but Chris was right— it was a monster, edging over our deck and branching out wildly, with more dead stuff underneath than green on top.

Chris had taken a look at similar junipers in the neighbourhood (as I said earlier, it was a popular shrub when these houses were built) and noted that some had been trimmed bonsai style. He took me, bemused by his sudden interest, on a walk around a few streets to see what others had done.

"Yes, that's worth a try," I said. "It may not make the juniper a beauty, but it will sure clean it up." We spent the next weekend clothed from head to toe (for there's no other way to work under a lethal old juniper, whose foliage, dead or alive, will leave you with welts from its nasty little points), clipping out dead wood and trimming back the limbs smoothly.

It was transformed. A sophisticated piece of artwork it had become, looking like an ancient tree in a Japanese painting. It looked so artistic even the fellow we later hired to put in garden lighting insisted we highlight it from below to make it a focal point.

This development was the first sign of Chris's new interest in the garden. Next was his hard work implementing my designer friend's plan for a revised back garden after the house renovation was completed. Chris says this wasn't significant, but I noticed the nuances: he initiated the work, going out after supper or early Saturday mornings without me so much as dropping a hint. His actions may not seem like much, but every woman will appreciate what I'm saying.

Re-doing the pathway was hard, slogging work and required digging out the pea gravel and the limestone-screenings base from the original path and sitting area, laying down new landscape liner to follow the revamped shapes, digging in the brick edging so that it was level and high enough to hold in the gravel, and replacing and topping up the gravel. We skimmed off the sod for the expanded garden bed and tossed it behind the Norway maple, where it joined the excavated soil from the house renovation and gradually broke down to create a small berm. Then we dug new soil into the central bed. We laid the stepping stone path through it, with me supervising its curves and the fit of the stones and Chris doing the grunt work. It was fun working together.

Choosing a birdbath to be the garden's focal point was fun, too. We went to a place owned by a couple I'd met while researching an article for the magazine; they had a wide range of concrete cupids, gargoyles, wall plaques, and the like for sale, arranged over their country property as if it were in Pliny the Younger's garden. Chris wandered through the artifacts and finally chose his favourite. I deliberately abstained from making a choice while appearing to consider this one and that one, because I didn't want him to think he'd just come along for the ride. But an uncomfortable recollection crept into my mind: I remembered overhearing a neighbour telling Joe years earlier that he always let his wife choose the colour of the new car so that she'd feel she was part of the purchase, even when, of course, it would be *his* car. I thought it was a sexist, manipulative technique back then, but it seemed like a smart psychological move to me now. I waved away my guilty feelings and went with Chris's choice, which happily was a classic design with a fluted base.

Chris doesn't recognize these little markers, but they spoke to me. The turning point, the one he acknowledges as his real conversion to garden involvement, was the pond.

His one request when we were discussing the garden's redesign was a pond and the sound of water. So that the sound could be enjoyed as we sat on the deck, my friend had worked into the plan the elegant three-foot-square pond set flush into one end; this he centred with a large stone that supports a Japanese deer scarer similar to the one suggested years before by the young meadow man; maybe he was ahead of his time. A deer scarer is difficult to describe in words, but essentially it is a bamboo pipe that pivots on a support; water supplied by a hollowed-out bamboo spout, set outside the pond, runs into the mouth of the pipe; when the pipe fills it tips forward, the water runs out in a little gurgle and the pipe falls backward to tap on the stone. (This is what scares away the deer, and it works, by the way: we have no deer in our garden.) It makes a pleasant, clear sound, but the intermittent rush of the water leaving the pipe and the small *tap* was not exactly what Chris had in mind. "I was hoping for a larger pond with the sound of a waterfall," he said. "Maybe I'll have to make one."

This proclamation struck fear into my heart, coming from a man who had trouble putting the barbecue back together after he'd cleaned it. And a waterfall? On our perfectly flat lot? How would he do that? I had visions of a stone cairn jutting up on a windswept landscape, but I didn't want to dampen his new enthusiasm for the garden. So I adopted my bad-hairstyle philosophy (it's only hair, and it will grow out) and agreed that he should go for it.

One Friday evening a taxi dropped me off when I returned from a garden-scouting trip to the east coast for the magazine. Chris had left me a message to say that something had come up and he wouldn't be able to pick me up at the airport, and I had assumed it was a football practice. But when I walked around to the backyard, there he was, nearly waist deep in what had been one of my perennial beds at the back of the garden.

"Hi!" he called, a big grin on his face. "Sorry I couldn't pick you up. But I'm digging a pond, and I want to finish it this weekend."

He managed to get the liner installed before sundown Sunday, and over the next two weekends he added a rock edging and a natural pebble shoreline, plus a waterfall just the right height for a soothing gurgle over a perfectly placed drip stone. The hose connected to the recirculating pump was cunningly hidden in the rockery and the plants he'd spent hours selecting at the nursery. It fit together beautifully and almost looked as if it had been placed in the corner of our garden by Mother Nature herself.

We've spent many an enjoyable hour beside Chris's pond, and he spends nearly as much time tending to the fish and the plants as I do deadheading and weeding. The fish—orange comets and black, white, and orange shebunkins—which Chris knows individually, according to their colour combinations, have had many babies over the years that have been adopted out to ponding friends. They winter over in the deepest water in the centre, and a small pond heater prevents total freeze-over.

Just like a gardener, Chris decided a couple of years ago that he needed more space—for his pond. So out went the handful of spiky blue grass plants and the purple coneflower, which had been taking over the small growing space around the original pond anyway, and in went a new pond twice the size of the first one. It's a definite improvement, and he did it with no prompting from me.

"GARDENING IS AN ART, just as painting is an art, and it's not likely that two people will collaborate happily in creating [a] garden." So wrote the eighty-five-year-old Emily Whaley in her 1997 memoir, *Mrs. Whaley and Her Charleston Garden*. Emily (Chukka to her friends) had a wealthy husband who wasn't himself interested in gardening but appreciated a fine one, with a good balance of colours, shapes, light, and shadow. He and Emily enjoyed a long and happy marriage and entertained often in their garden because Emily loved to cook and believed that gardens were for sharing. I do wish I'd had the chance to meet her, but she died the year after her memoir was published. Her plot was smallish for a grand garden—only 30 by 110 feet behind the family's narrow clapboard house and divided into five areas filled with large azalea and camellia shrubs, hydrangeas and roses, plus a constantly blooming array of perennials and annuals, among them day lilies, pansies, and gerbera daisies—but it was for years a fixture on Charleston's historic garden tours, even after her death; sometimes it accommodated as many as three thousand visitors a year.

Emily definitely had a point about collaboration. It's hard to share the creative process, in a garden or anywhere else. But although making a garden may not be a team sport, it helps to have a partner. You do need help once your knees have started to give out, or when the flagstones are too heavy to lift. Uncle Ren gardened alone, but he did have the benefit of farm equipment to help him in times of need.

Emily had Junior Robinson, her loyal gardener. "[He's] the perfect assistant... enthusiastic, optimistic, and patient," she wrote in her memoir. "He says whatever we do together is as much fun for him as it is for me. He moves around the flower borders like a cat, never disturbing a plant. It's a rare accomplishment and the first prerequisite you must look for in anyone engaged to help in your garden."

The original design of Emily's garden was a gift from her husband while she was confined to bed in 1941 with a difficult pregnancy. He asked what would make her feel better, and she had a quick answer: a garden design, by the best landscape architect South Carolina could offer, a certain Loutrel Briggs. He created the garden rooms and some brick dividing walls, all designed to capitalize on the placement of the mighty oaks and magnolia trees in the background. Then Emily took over. Over the years Junior was kept busy working alongside her as she renovated and re-renovated the garden, adding and removing statuary and trying new plant combinations as her tastes changed.

She admitted her style of gardening needed an ample supply of money, and she advised choosing a husband carefully. "A good and generous man is needed," she wrote, "one who knows how to make money and enjoys sharing it." But one who prefers to remain uninvolved in the making of the garden. To make it up to her husband for staying in his own territory and for his generosity, she allowed him to cast her votes for any office that should be on a ballot, from dogcatcher to president, and she always had custard in the refrigerator.

Vita Sackville-West and her husband, Harold Nicolson, two of the most famous gardeners of the twentieth century, worked as a couple, and they kept the peace by dividing the creative process. They had more than one Junior to help them; they had more than twenty. They were of the aristocracy, after all—Vita, the daughter of a baron, was an author and poet, and Harold was a diplomat, journalist, and member of Parliament. Both were serious gardeners, having started their first one in Kent, England, in 1915; they bought Sissinghurst Castle, also in Kent and now the destination of choice for North American gardeners touring England, in 1930. It was a ruin when they purchased it, but they transformed it together, turning it into a series of hedged or walled enclosures, each garden with a different theme or colour and reflecting Vita's informal approach to planting, including her white garden. It was a model for many gardeners, including me, in the early '90s.

My white garden was an utter failure. Many supposedly white cultivars I chose so carefully at the nursery didn't come true to form—a new white coneflower bloomed the common purple-pink, and the common white baby's breath I really wanted turned out to be a new pink type. This occurrence isn't uncommon for gardeners, and I'm sure it's easy for growers to mislabel plants or for labels to get mixed up at the nursery, but it's frustrating when you're trying to create a certain colour scheme. I gave up on my white garden and let it revert to whatever colours it wanted to be, but Vita's, started in the '50s, was—and is—a

125

knockout. It's a pale mix of grey, silver, and white flowering and foliage plants (with a few touches of yellow) designed to complement each other in shape and texture and to glow at twilight, when it's best seen by visitors, although most tour it when bright sunshine washes out its pale tones. In fact, Vita planned it as a dining garden, to look its best at the end of the day. Many grey and silver foliage plants form a muted underplanting: several varieties of artemisias with feathery or lobe-shaped leaves, including wormwood, the source of absinthe (that favourite potion of Paris bohemians of the late nineteenth and early twentieth centuries); and low mounds of grey santolina, more colourfully known as lavender cotton or holy herb. Tall, nodding white columbine or dense spires of foxglove poke through the undergrowth; pure white calla lilies, white tree peonies and foamy baby's breath add their own different textures. A clump of eight-foot-tall, silvery-leaved Arabian thistle commands an area, and clusters of the white blooms of a huge *Rosa mulliganii* sprawl over a central arbour, the plant carefully pruned so that it doesn't hide the arbour's lines.

Harold and Vita did not tread on each other's toes in the garden. Each had a territory according to his or her talents: Harold designed the layout, and Vita handled the plants. Harold's design, inspired by the gardens at Hidcote Manor in Gloucestershire, has a sophisticated sense of space, and Vita's plant choices reveal her romantic visual sense and her skill as a gardener. She was so dedicated to plants that once she spent all the prize money she won for an epic poem on azaleas for her garden.

Harold and Vita may also have been the most famous bisexuals in England. They enjoyed an open marriage with many affairs with persons of their own gender; it was a marriage that lasted for fifty years and provided both of them with emotional security and social comfort, plus two sons. The marriage would be unusual today; one can imagine how it was viewed then, even fifty years ago. But they were devoted to each other and created one of the most admired and influential gardens of the century. It's now owned by Britain's National Trust and is open to visitors.

Just like the affluent or celebrated gardening couples I've read about, the non-famous ones I know, including Chris and me, also go their own way in the garden unless four arms and two backs are required for a specific job. Some couples divide the chores and some divide the garden; I can't recall couples who work closely together on every garden project. Garden writer Des Kennedy, whom I count as one of my friends, gardens with enthusiasm and style on Denman Island, B.C., and confers with his wife, Sandy, on big changes before they're initiated, but then they separate to do their own work. Sandy generally handles the ornamentals—the planting, weeding, dividing, and dead-heading—and Des looks after trees, fruits and vegetables, and digging, pruning, and compost. Another couple I know who are both interested in design and plants divides the areas—he designed, planted, and maintains the large, lovely rock and scree garden; she planned and carried out the formal perennial garden, with a little help from their own particular part-time Junior. These divisions usually come about quite naturally as a result of each gardener's personal interest.

I'm loath to think that gardeners fall into such stereotypes, but some generalizations can't be avoided: more often the garden responsibilities are divided up according to the male–female brawn–brains division. Almost without exception the woman handles the pretty stuff and the man does the heavy work. I suppose there's some logic to that arrangement. I've certainly never seen a clear-cut case of the reverse, although a dear friend of mine always cut the grass and pruned the shrubs, while her husband tended the vegetable garden. They didn't grow flowers.

Other stereotypes abound. Long ago, and I'm thinking particularly of the Renaissance and later, since we know little about the designers of gardens of the Middle Ages, men were the only garden architects, and they were highly respected for their work. Men like Leon Battista Alberti and Donato Bramante; they designed expansive and elaborate gardens for the Medicis and various popes, and we're still reading about their power and influence in the world of garden design. Another example is André Le Nôtre, who planned the gardens at Versailles for Louis XIV, and let's not overlook William Kent and Capability Brown, the fathers of the Landscape Movement. And there are many more men in their ranks.

Where were the women? Planting flowers? Even Gertrude Jekyll, who had a successful business partnership with Edward Lutyens a century ago, specialized in colour coordinating the flowerbeds while he designed the garden architecture.

But I suppose I'm tilting at windmills. The world of garden design has been no different from the world of government, business, and cooking, to suggest only three fields where men have dominated for hundreds of years. But the times they are a-changin', and soon you might see me out there up to my knees in the pond, while Chris plants the posies.

It occurs to me that Chris's interest in the garden over the years has increased as his athletic skills decreased. Could there possibly be a connection? A hamstring pull here, chronic Achilles tendonitis or a torn rotator cuff there... and there... and there. They've all contributed in a curious way to making his garden chores more palatable. This past fall, after an injury-filled year of touch football and only a couple of touchdowns, he announced it might be time to retire.

Well, I've heard that one before, and perhaps too late I realize he's been planning this move and phasing in golf to fill the void football will leave in his life.

Believe me, I'm not questioning the process—as my joints are replaced one by one with shiny new titanium ones, I've been thinking of replacing some of the perennials in the garden with lower-maintenance shrubs. And if gardening takes second place in Chris's list of enjoyable divertissements, that works for me— especially if he further hones his area of specialty: pruning.

Chris is a master pruner. I think without realizing it he somehow communes with the tree or shrub before he even picks up his saw or pruner. I think he studies them carefully and asks each untidy plant just what it needs to make it grow more strongly and look more beautiful. A severe thinning? Perhaps just a little off the top? A complete reshaping? He envisions the final look— a graceful vase shape, perhaps an arching fountain; yes, even a bonsai trim. Then out comes the curved Japanese saw and the secateurs. An hour or so later we have a revitalized dogwood or a rarin'-to-go deutzia.

I clip the foot-tall boxwood hedges I planted to curve around the thyme bed in the back garden, but I don't tread on Chris's territory. The shrubs and small trees—never the huge Norway maple, it's in the hands of an arbourist—are left for his hands.

Chris has become an integral part of this garden, in its upkeep, of course, but also in the way the plants and the design are evolving, so I figured I should show him the first draft of this book and ask if he had any comments.

"Just one," he said, after skimming through it. "I notice you say 'my garden' this and 'my garden' that. Shouldn't that be 'our garden'?"

I think that's all the proof you or I need that we have indeed become partners in the garden.

129

❦

CHAPTER 10

Screening

THE GARDEN

. . . . .

ANYONE WATCHING lifestyle television these days might think that redecorating your neighbours' family room over a weekend while they do yours has taken over from gardening as the hobby of the new millennium, and they may be right. Personally, I don't think so, but who am I to say? I know little about how television networks make their decisions, whether they're based on what polls say listeners want or what the TV executives *think* they want, but a couple of requirements seem obvious: a potential show must reveal more about the hosts than the subject, and each episode must always feature a crisis, such as a fireplace mantel that's come up two inches short or a wall colour that turns out to be hideous and has to be repainted with only seconds to the show's end. Garden shows barely exist today, and when they do the gardens are decorated, not planted.

Well, that's my rant. During the '90s, when gardening and not home decorating was the hot topic, I had my own three-year brush with a television show, and it taught me more than I had known before, and not just about television. (I enjoyed almost every minute of it, by the way.) The idea germinated in 1996, when one of the lifestyle networks that now focus on home-decorating shows knocked on *Canadian Gardening*'s door. They wanted to do a magazine-style gardening show, and who better to help them than a gardening magazine?

The publishing company's new editorial director and I, wearing my best suit and fresh from the hairstylist, met with network brass and the head of the production company in the late winter of that year to discuss the idea. We came to a quick philosophical accord, financial details to be worked out later: they knew how to produce a TV show, and we had the gardening knowledge to help make it happen. The show would carry the magazine's name and broaden our market ("expand the franchise" was the term bandied about), and we would provide the production company with ideas and contacts to create a show with several segments—a tour of someone's garden, a how-to project, a garden technique, a plant portrait, that sort of thing. It was a win-win situation (that term was used, too).

The burning question: did anyone have any idea who would make a good host?

Why do you suppose I was wearing my best outfit and freshly coiffed hair?

I'd had a few minor experiences with microphones and public appearances in my life, the most significant being Suzy's wedding reception, for which she'd asked if I would like to give a short speech. Yes, certainly, I said. I prepared a six-sentence address with a couple of loving jokes at Suzy's expense and a welcome to all the guests. I was so nervous I tripped over the mike cord on my way to the podium and a made a little off-the-cuff joke about what a klutz I was. The guests laughed. They laughed at my speech, too. I was charmed. I loved it. I wanted more.

The gardening show looked like my big chance. I modestly offered my services, assuring the group I wouldn't be the least bit insulted if they thought I might not be the right person, or if I showed no talent in front of a camera, or—this said to the editorial director—if it conflicted with my real job as editor of the magazine.

This offer sat silently on the table for a minute or so, during which I wished I'd kept my mouth shut, then someone said that I'd have to audition for the job, but of course I'd be seriously considered. The group acknowledged that I already had a persona connected to the magazine that an actor would not have and that this fact might go over well with viewers.

My audition consisted of a pleasant visit to my garden by one of the producers, a nice man who made me feel confident that I could ace this audition.

"Just show me around your garden and tell me about it," he said. "I'll follow you with the camera and get all the right angles. Don't worry about me, but do remember not to look at me but down the barrel."

This was a term I'd hear often the first year of shooting, and the gun reference struck me as apt. It's intimidating to have to look at your own faint reflection in a disc of glass at the barrel end of a video camera, instead of at the human being holding the apparatus. It's a little like talking to yourself.

But I wasn't at a loss for words during the audition; talking about the garden I knew so well was easy. It was fun, in fact. I kept walking and talking, with the producer following as he'd promised, shooting me and them zooming down to focus on the plant I was referring to, or following my gesture to take in the arbour and the New Dawn rose. Finally he said "Cut!" and I was almost sorry it was over.

I got the job. I probably got it primarily because the show was partnered by the magazine, but *c'est la vie.* They accepted me, so I didn't ask questions. The producers decided that I would introduce and close the show (known as doing the "intros" and "extros") and do the opening garden visit with the garden owner as well as some of the how-to projects.

Doing the job turned out not to be nearly as easy as acing the audition.

Canadian Gardening Television started shooting in Toronto early in the summer of '96 for a launch in winter '97. We had a decidedly professional crew: a director-producer, sound and camera people, a production assistant, and sometimes more, depending on what we were doing; most were regulars on serious stuff like documentaries and movies. Even if they didn't know one another well they operated as the proverbial happy family, as you have to when you're working closely together to meet the day's deadline with the ever-present challenges of the outdoors, and they were almost universally supportive of the amateur in their midst. Over the summer and into the fall we taped segments in other parts of Canada. The crews changed from week to week, depending on who was available, but by the second and third years we had a fairly regular group.

I thought magazine editors laboured long and hard, but we had nothing on these television people. We worked literally from dawn to dusk in order to catch the right light, avoiding the too-bright periods at midday and shooting every scene several times from different positions so that it could be edited for a variety of angles and maintain the continuity. But what do you do when the neighbour's air-conditioner starts up just as you're asking the gardener the name of that white lily, or when the sun disappears behind the clouds mid-scene, only to reappear thirty seconds later as you're doing a cloudy retake? Why, you start again, my dears—several times if need be. If it rains you sit in the car or on the gardener's veranda waiting for the sky to clear, and you don't declare it a washout until it rains for a couple of

133

hours—misty or lightly overcast days, however, can be lovely for shooting gardens, as I knew from attending magazine photo sessions. If it's cold, you wear long underwear under your nifty TV garden outfit and shiver under a coat when you're off camera.

Promptly at noon we'd head en masse to a local restaurant for exactly an hour's lunch, and we took two breaks a day, fifteen minutes each, with coffee and Danishes brought in by the production assistant. There must be a union rule in there somewhere. To shoot an eight-minute garden visit took about eight hours, and after I got home or back to the hotel I'd collapse into a deep sleep, if only for half an hour.

This was hard work, and I learned not to complain about my arthritic knee and to willingly do a botched take yet again without even the slightest sigh. I learned to look blindly into the sun and ignore my stinging eyes. And I tried hard to smile while passing on ordinary instructions to the camera, like "Dip the brush into the thin black wash, let it drain for a few seconds, then brush it generously over the urn, letting the black paint run where it wants to. It will go into the hollows and mix with the green paint, and the urn will look like it's a hundred years old when it's dry."

This wasn't the sort of statement I ordinarily made with a big smile, and it's hard to speak clearly while grinning broadly, but I was assured that a constant smile was crucial for TV. I'm afraid I kept reverting to smileless normalcy too often, and the production assistant finally made a big sign to hold up: two grinning red lips, with one jagged tooth in the centre. When I saw it I *had* to smile.

This exercise did teach me the power of a smile, however. I began to adopt a big smile wherever I went, except while walking by myself down the street, of course. I'd smile when asking for service or directions or making a complaint, and I found that people responded more readily. Sometimes people suspect you're about to hurl criticism or anger their way, and they get their dukes up. When you smile you disarm them. A smile puts everyone in a friendlier mood and leaves a good feeling all around, even if you're just asking the way to the loo.

As the season's shooting continued I became more relaxed and confident about my role as host, but it became clear I had another hole in my talent bag: I wasn't a quick study, as they say in the acting business. I had trouble remembering my lines, especially if someone else had written them for me. I didn't have a problem strolling with someone through his or her garden and asking questions or commenting on this or that; that seemed like natural discourse, and in the garden visits I was pretty well free to conduct my own interview as long as I covered the necessary points. But memorize five lines to intro the show, or ten to explain a method like aging an urn? Several takes later I could be a basket case of dithering nerves.

It's easy for a grown woman to feel like a scared ten-year-old when several pairs of eyes are on her, the camera is rolling, and she's flubbed her lines five times already, and this is where the supportive crew came in. One would make a joke, another would call for a pee break, the tension would ease, and the action would roll again. But one of the producer-directors clearly didn't suffer amateurs gladly (you did note my "almost universally" comment above, didn't you?), and her displeasure when I stumbled over my lines was palpable. A couple of times I wanted to fall down sobbing or give up and go home immediately, but I realized that would be actually acting like a ten-year-old. So I'd try the deep-breathing techniques I'd learned long ago in yoga. As I was counting and slowly exhaling, the camera and soundmen would catch my eye and give me a thumbs up and a big smile, and soon I'd be able to carry on.

The lesson hit home: support and positive feedback produce better results than criticism, even if the criticism is only implied. My grandmother was right; you can catch more flies with honey. This producer-director's curling lip was definitely vinegar, as well as cruelly defeating. I remembered to opt for the honey approach when dealing with nervous gardeners I was interviewing, although there were few of them—most basked in the idea that *Canadian Gardening Television* was filming their garden and welcomed us with open arms and nary a shred of anxiety.

During the three years we spent taping *Canadian Gardening Television*, I spent hours with dozens of gardeners all across Canada, chatting between takes and getting to know them— this helped them stay relaxed and gave me more insight into their garden goals, which of course enhanced our on-camera visits. These conversations confirmed my impression that gardeners have a lot in common. For example, many tend to anthropomorphize plants, a lovely big word I'd never try to pronounce on TV that simply means we attribute human qualities to inanimate things. I'm guilty to a degree—in my head certain plants in my garden are defenceless children or sophisticated ladies, but I've never referred to them that way out loud. Plenty of gardeners do, and Uncle Ren was one of them. He had a gorgeous, award-winning red rose he always referred to as "she," and any cobalt-blue delphinium was invariably called "he," although the pink and white ones were girls. His grafted apples were male. "Don't eat that one—he's got a worm!" I distinctly remember him cautioning me one long-ago summer as I was about to bite into a juicy red fruit. I remember one TV guest whose white lilies were female and the red ones male. References like these seemed more or less normal to me, but an east coast woman took it further. "Look at those handsome boys down there," she said to me proudly when I visited her garden. I thought she was referring to her grandsons. "Aren't they just perfect?" When I followed her gaze and there were no children down there, I must have looked puzzled. She was embarrassed. "Oh, I'm so sorry; I do that all the time, and people don't know what I'm talking about. I mean that bed of evergreens in the corner."

Our arbourist does this, too, and he's a professional. He always calls our big Norway maple "he," and our apple trees were "the old girls." He attended the deathbeds of the apple trees (trimming their trunks and branches into fireplace lengths so that we could remember them all winter) and is now nursing the Norway maple through its geriatric years. But his tendency to, um, give trees human attributes stood out when he made an emergency call last year to look at our smoke tree.

The smoke tree grows close to the kitchen addition; it was there before the new kitchen and the expanded deck, and it shades the deck; we didn't want to remove it, so we left a slot to accommodate it, but it's lost a few limbs over the years. It's nearly thirty years old now, and its remaining single limb was leaning forward at an alarming angle and rubbing against the house in the wind, making a sound like a creaking four-master in a storm. We called the arbourist in to see if we could do anything to support the tree, or whether it was even worth saving. Very seriously he palpated the limbs, checked the bark and the splits in a couple of branches. He pulled off a leaf and examined it. "Well, she's old," he finally said. "But she's pretty healthy compared with similar trees her age. There's no reason to cut her down—I think all she needs is a good support to straighten her up a bit."

I imagined an oversized cane, or an arboreal version of one of those wheel-and-sit contraptions. He described a collar to cradle the limb and a cable to support the collar, attached firmly to a block of wood inserted between two beams of the arbour.

137

"But is she, I mean, it, healthy enough to last a few more years?" I asked.

"Look at it this way," he replied. "She's like an old but healthy lady. You can see two eighty-year-old women side by side, and one can be all bent over and really diseased, and the other might be bent over too and have a few scars, but generally she's healthy. That's her."

Just as the arbourist felt the nooks and crannies of the smoke tree, I've seen gardeners poke about their plants with the authority of a doctor feeling for a lump in a breast. I've seen gardeners pull off a leaf and scrape the scale on the underside with their fingernails, then sniff it. I've seen them sniff the soil and roughly loosen or cut the tightly curled roots of a plant they're transplanting because they know this is what the roots need so that they can spread and grow into their new home.

Uncle Ren had done these things, and perhaps I do, too. Perhaps it has something to do with understanding your plants, the way Chris studies a shrub he's about to prune before he picks up his saw. Perhaps it's the gardeners' way to attribute some kind of life they can identify with to their plants so that they can do right by them. In his book *Second Nature*, Michael Pollan writes enchantingly about getting into the heads of the unhappy, stumpy carrots in his garden so that he could figure out what they wanted to grow properly. "This is not as dumb a question as it sounds," he writes. "It is more than an anthropomorphic conceit to attribute likes and dislikes to plants, to wonder, if not about how they're 'feeling,' then at least about what matters to them, what they require in order to fulfill the terms of their destiny."

I laughed as I read about how he pictured the environment under the surface of his carrot patch as the ". . . Number 6 train at rush hour, jammed with cramped orange commuters. My carrots stood too close together; I had been insufficiently ruth-less. . . thinning the seedlings."

In his mind's eye, Pollan imagined something else: happier, more thinned carrots stretching and growing, driving their newly freed carroty selves straight down into softer, more fri-able soil. To fulfill their destinies carrots need airy soil, and a good poke with his index finger revealed thick clay a couple of inches under the surface. So he renovated the carrots' bed the next spring by digging in builder's sand, peat moss, and com-post, and then as the carrots sprouted he thinned the population rigorously so that each had its own seat on the train. By August, he writes, he was pulling up some of the longest, handsomest carrots he'd ever seen. He was earning his green thumb through trial and error.

And thus arises once again the controversial idea of the green thumb, or Russell Page's "green fingers." Not many gardeners could be so imaginative in describing how they finally achieved success with carrots, or roses or lilies, but, as Pollan points out, getting into a plant's head and learning what it needs may be what a green thumb is really all about. If it isn't born into you—which, let's face it, it likely isn't, or my sister Bobbie might have been a serious gardener too, but she showed little interest in growing things—it may be achieved by reading good garden books or watching TV garden shows (which you could do if any of them were around anymore), or swapping stories with other gardeners. My arbourist knows about trees because he has a degree in for-estry and years of experience dealing with diseased and injured ones in people's backyards. He's earned his green thumb.

And now we shall abandon the discussion of green thumbs because, as I said before, we'll never resolve it. I think it's accepted among gardeners, however, that we do share many traits. Most of us love to cook and to eat (and this I don't have a theory about) and many paint or take artistic photographs, but these last two could spring from an interest in preserving the garden for posterity. Most gardeners are young for their years, staying flexible and vigorous, busy and active. Gardeners can talk, too. Whatever our differences with regard to politics, religion, or age, all the ones I've met could talk non-stop about gardening. We're on the same wavelength. I remember a woman who was eighty-four years old when I met her in her Nova Scotia garden nearly fifteen years ago; she'd been tending her patch since 1940 with little time to sit on her front porch because there was always something to do, and she insisted I take home with me a root of her vanilla-scented valerian. We must have spent a couple of hours talking without pause, comparing notes about our respective gardens. She grew vegetables and strawberries on one side of her long front yard and flowers on the other. The produce went to friends and neighbours, the flowers to the church on Sundays. When she and her husband built the house, the front yard had been a sunken hole that constantly filled with water. For a few years the kids used it as a rink; then it was filled in with great quantities of seaweed and manure and became a fine garden.

I did venture into a non-gardening topic with another octogenarian gardener, at least on a superficial level. A retired university scientist, he lectured internationally on chaos theory and told me there was hidden symmetry in the world and that it was governed by the laws of chaos. At least I think that's what he said. I was interested in the subject, and we explored it until he realized how far it was beyond me, and then we went back to gardening. He started seedlings in a little greenhouse and planted flowers in gently curving beds because he said that in nature you never find straight lines and flowers set in rows. That I *could* understand.

Most gardeners are people like these—friendly, sharing, down-to-earth. Many are young and enthusiastic, but lots, as I said, are a bit on in years, too, and this gives me comfort; it's proof that having an interest beyond yourself and keeping physically busy supports longevity. But I've run into a few of the superior sort of gardener, people who look down their noses if you pronounce campanula as "cam-pan-oo-la" instead of "cam-PAN-you-la," considered the correct way in horticultural circles. There was the woman who thought her garden too good for *Canadian Gardening*. "You can come to see it," she said (I'm sure she'd rather have said "admire"), "but my garden will never appear in your magazine." I didn't bother to visit. And some gardeners can be perfectionists, such as my friend the surgeon who measures the distances between plants as if he's doing a lobotomy. Perfectionists tend to make messy gardeners like me feel quite inadequate, especially when their gardens look as spontaneously elegant as his does.

Perfection, perhaps, is in the eye of the beholder. Some gardeners are militant about removing every leaf from their gardens in fall, and some are not. I'm in the latter category: I rather like to see a few red and gold leaves lying naturally on my gravel path where a warm fall breeze blew them. I think that's why I enjoyed the anecdote I read in Henry Mitchell's book, *One Man's Garden*, about a certain Lady Rothschild who some years ago was visiting an ordinary person's garden. Her own garden was flawlessly neat, courtesy of a staff of gardeners, with nothing ever out of place; in the garden she was visiting brightly coloured leaves were scattered on the paths. The Lady was impressed. "How lovely," she said. "I presume you have them imported?"

THERE WERE some changes made for the second and third seasons of *Canadian Gardening Television*—a co-host was brought in, a likable young man with lots of energy and on-camera experience. At first I felt a tiny bit rejected and wondered if this was the beginning of the end for me; I was still learning this TV racket and enjoying it immensely, despite the hard work (I was still in charge of the magazine as well, with much necessary support from its long-suffering staff). But the producers were souls of diplomacy, explaining how adding a touch of youth, especially virile male youth, would be a shot of adrenalin for the show and complement my gardening experience, which appealed to many viewers. I could accept that, even if they might have been saying that they wanted a younger, hotter host with more television pizzazz.

The change turned out to be a positive one—I liked my co-host, Kevin Brauch, and we worked well together, doing all the intros and extros in my garden. My neighbours were understanding—they didn't object to all the action even when we asked if they wouldn't mind not using the leaf blower today because it ruined our sound continuity. The kids next door loved it. Kevin was a featured performer on an after-school kids' TV show, and they and their buddies would peer through the fence watching their idol in action. As for me, I was just the woman who hired them now and again to water her container plants when she was out of town. Occasionally we'd ask them over for a close look from the sidelines. After a few takes of the same scene, they generally got bored and went home.

My garden suffered a bit from all the action. I learned not to cringe when the cameraman had to walk backward though the perennials to get just the right angle as Kevin and I strolled down the path chatting about the show viewers were about to see, and I learned to take a fresh look at my garden through the eyes of the set decorator. Sometimes he brought in chairs or tables or other props I would never have chosen and put them places I never would have thought of putting them. He moved my teak garden bench from its boring old place in the rear sitting area to under the Norway maple. No one ever sat on it anyway, partly because it's not as comfortable as it might be, but in its new place it took on more importance: it became a focal point, as seen from the kitchen window. It sits there still.

Also remaining in the garden from the glory days of TV is a mirror built into a fake arbour, which we erected under the Norway maple for a how-to project. It startles new visitors. They think it's the entrance to another part of the garden until they see their reflection approaching, and then there's an *Oh!* moment. Not only is it a good example of *trompe l'oeil,* but it's also a conversation piece.

After three years and over sixty half-hour segments, the network decided not to renew the show. It had been fun, as well as a learning experience, but it was over. Before we wound down, however, I had an unintentional surprise.

During a story meeting the researcher described a garden she'd found in mid-Toronto that would make a good garden visit for me. "It's not big," she said, "but it's beautifully designed and kept by one of the women who owns a mail-order bulb company in Toronto. Lots of roses, miniature lilacs, smelly plants like that... There's a great pond in a walled garden, and the house is old and lovely." She went on to describe the location. *I used to live in that neighbourhood when I first came to Toronto,* I thought. *Maybe I'll have a chance to check out my old boarding house.*

The house *was* my old boarding house, magically returned to its original glory as a single-family dwelling. I couldn't believe it when the crew and I drove up the morning of the shoot—I was rendered nearly speechless. The garden was smaller, because years earlier the rose garden had been sold off to make a lot for a skinny townhouse, but there was a lovely new walled garden at the back, one strollable enough for a whole cast of Jane Austen characters.

143

It also turned out that I was already acquainted with the woman I was to interview: a year before, we'd enjoyed each other's company and a pleasant chat about our avocations at a book launch at her small garden shop, Cruickshank's, in midtown Toronto, the same shop from which Uncle Ren and I had once ordered bulbs and exotica, including gifts for each other at Christmas. I never would have guessed at the time that she lived in my old boarding house.

And here I was, interviewing her for the garden show and taking a nostalgic tour through my former abode. It seemed a serendipitous visit for our last year of shooting.

❦

CHAPTER 11

The

CALL OF THE WILD

· · · · ·

B Y THE TIME we started to tape *Canadian Gardening Television* in '96, our new front garden was pretty well established and offered a diversity of locations for the intro and extro parts we did on our property. The front is filled with perennials, roses, and shrubs and had become a veritable wildlife preserve alive with winged creatures, creepy crawlies, and lots of four-footed creatures. This includes our own cats and the neighbourhood felines, which masquerade as lions and prowl the make-believe jungle as if it's their own. All these creatures had formerly confined themselves to the back garden, but doubling the garden's size and increasing its biodiversity effectively doubled their population.

I'm sure you've heard about the importance of biodiversity. A biodiverse garden contains more than just many different plants—it's also home to a variety of birds that eat seeds and then disperse them over the landscape, good bugs that duke it out with the bad bugs and keep them under control, butterflies and bees that pollinate the plants. In other words, a biodiverse garden preserves the balance of nature. And the first thing you usually notice in such a garden is the abundance of birds. Our garden—indeed, our whole neighbourhood, because of its many trees and shrubs—is home to dozens of species and a destination for many others as they stop for food and water on their way to their winter or summer homes.

Birds are a joy in the garden, especially in the winter, when their flitting about the backyard feeders (we have two) brings life to an otherwise bleak landscape and drives our cats wild from inside the French doors; we keep a weather eye on them when they go outside, although the birds are generally much faster than the cats. Gorgeous cardinals come in pairs to the feeder—we have two loyal couples that dine there frequently, sometimes bringing their teenagers along. Chris and I always listen for the male's *cue cue cue cue cheer cheer cheer cheer cheer* in late winter—it tells us spring really is going to show up soon, no matter how dreary the days may seem at the moment. In summer I try to whistle back when I hear the cardinal's long, liquid call, and most times he replies, with exactly the same number of *cheer cheers*, but I think he's testing me because I know I don't sound like a cardinal, and soon he abandons the game.

At various times purple finches, sparrows, the bossy blue jay, who muscles other birds aside in his greedy quest for food, gold finches, and grackles visit the feeder. Mourning doves perambulate around on the ground in their slightly dazed way, and the smart, perky robins search for worms once the snow melts. In early fall large flocks of noisy little sparrows eat the seeds of the cedars growing between our house and our neighbour's. They shriek their delight at such a fine array of food and yak to each other as they share the meal. If I should open the back door even a crack, and as noiselessly as I can, silence instantly falls. I guess I'm a threat, although all I really want to do is get a closer look.

We've seen many a generation of birds raised in our garden. Birds have nested in the hollows of our now-gone apple trees and in the branches of the Norway maple, and they have taken up residence in our birdhouses. We watch as the parents lovingly— and constantly—feed the babies, train them to fly and then kick them out. Normally they seem oblivious to their audience, but not the aggressive and suspicious blue jays. One summer evening I was sitting on the edge of the deck idly watching a pair of them create a ruckus in the Norway maple. *What are they up to?* I wondered. *Jay jay jay!* they called angrily. *Jay jay jay!* Wings bristled and feathers flew as they pranced around and bristled their feathers.

It's mad passion or a darned good fight, I thought.

Then one took off and headed my way. *She's flounced off in a temper.* But it was me she was angry with. She headed straight for me, flying low and fast, and grazed the top of my head. She turned and headed back towards me. I got up and ran into the house, visions of Alfred Hitchcock's *The Birds* in my head. It wasn't till I reached the safety of the kitchen and looked out the window that I saw the juveniles, flying shakily from a low limb of the maple to the roof of my neighbour's shed. The fight had been a diversionary tactic.

I always marvel at the intelligence of birds and their family togetherness.

147

OUR STREET is also home to hundreds (it seems) of four-footed creatures: squirrels, raccoons, plus a few skunk families. Sometimes an occasional opossum and a shy fox pass through on a quest for a few mice from the compost bins. Someone once claimed to see a coyote, but I think it was a lost dog, although coyotes have been seen a few miles from here on a hydro right-of-way near a wooded area and the river. It's the resident rodents that do the damage, seldom the visitors. I admit to ambivalent feelings about the squirrels and raccoons, but Chris and I like animals and generally hold the opinion that, within reason, they have as much right to the outdoors as we do, even when the outdoors happen to be our garden.

My neighbour, Mary, however, is a real softie—she puts out dishes of dry food and sometimes even cans of bargain-priced tuna for possible stray cats and hungry raccoons who just can't find anything really good to eat. I expect that's another good reason why we have so many resident animals and their dinner guests on our block; perhaps even the coyote got wind of the all-you-can-eat buffet. One year Mary leaned a ladder against an open first-floor window to accommodate one of her cats, who likes to come and go as he pleases at night; trouble was, a mother raccoon thought it was meant for her and her baby and paid my neighbour's living room a midnight visit.

I adore Mary; she's one of the kindest, most generous people I've ever met, even—maybe especially—when it comes to animals, and this puts her at one end of the ambivalence scale. I have a long-time friend who's at the other. She grew up on a farm and knows how to shoot a rifle—a long gun it's called in arms parlance—and she has the permit and ammunition to use it. She moved back to the country for a while a few years ago, and her farming instincts returned: in cold blood (at least that's my view—hers is different), she'd shoot any pesky little squirrel that jumped onto the flat bird feeder on the deck off her kitchen. Shoot it dead, with one well-aimed missile. I was horrified, but I was mostly raised in urban areas and don't share her farming frame of mind. I do remember that my uncles had their .22 rifles standing inside the door of the summer kitchen on the farm so that as they sat smoking on the back stoop they could pick off the groundhogs they spotted in the fields; this practice always shocked me. I also remember them chopping off the heads of chickens destined for Sunday dinner, then chasing them as the poor things ran headless around the farmyard. Believe me, this scene still comes to mind when I'm preparing a chicken to roast for supper, although it never seems to spoil my taste for the meal.

Another neighbour (she's moved away now) used to put open-face peanut butter sandwiches on her windowsill so that she could watch the squirrels from her kitchen table. I confess that for a while I'd invite the little rodents for a crumb and a chat when I was having a weekend lunch on the deck, but that stopped once they started climbing the back-door screen every Saturday at noon. They were *so cute* when they were waiting for a morsel of food beside me, with their little hands folded and looking me right in the eye, but they got too familiar.

I like to watch the aerial acrobatics of squirrels, and I admire their resourcefulness and intelligence, but I have been known to taste blood. I've lost many a crocus, snowdrop, and species tulip before they even had a chance to sprout, because they're planted shallowly and are within easy reach of the squirrel's digging fingers, but it's the desecration of a plant in full bloom that drives me mad. One May day when one of the little rodents rampaged through a planting of luscious pink tulips (Renown, if I remember correctly), I wished I had my friend's .22. I caught the squirrel in the act from inside the French doors, chomping down on its sixth tulip just behind the bloom and devouring exactly one inch of the tender green stems before moving on to the next one, leaving the already fading flowers to die on the ground. I rushed out screaming like a banshee, scooping up some pea gravel as I ran. That damn little squirrel stared at me boldly, timing its move perfectly, and took just one more bite of fresh stem before the gravel flew. It scampered quickly away to the safety of the Norway maple, where it *gnaagnaa*'d at me, waiting till I'd disappeared indoors before coming back to resume the meal.

Ruined tulips and excavated crocuses are one thing, but stolen pantyhose and nipped-off outdoor lights are another. (I now spray the crocus bulbs with rodent repellant before planting, by the way; the spray works pretty well for tulip flowers, too, but you have to repeat it every few days to keep it potent. Some people put down a line of cayenne pepper to teach the rodents a lesson, but this trick never worked for me. Of course, shooting the little pests is frowned upon unless you live on a farm.) Yes, I said pantyhose back there, *my* pantyhose, and my neighbour's too. We blamed their frequent disappearance from our clotheslines on a perverted lingerie thief, but it was just a resourceful squirrel looking for comfy lining for her nest. Chris discovered the stolen underpinnings when he climbed up to investigate the impressive nest tucked into a corner of the arbour at the side of our house. It was a castle among nests, an elaborate bowl-shaped structure made of interlaced twigs and leaves. And lining the bottom were several pairs of pantyhose, along with a handful of the tiny white lights I'd spent an afternoon lacing through the smoke tree for summer-evening ambience. She wanted them because they'd make nice toys for the kids, I guess.

Everyone complains about squirrels, but some have more reason to do so than others. In England and Scotland, as well as some parts of northern Italy, our friendly grey squirrel (*Sciurus carolinensis*, native to the eastern part of North America) is gradually replacing the smaller European red squirrel (*Sciurus vulgaris*). According to one estimate the greys outnumber the reds by 3 million to 130,000, although how they're counted is a puzzle to me. I can't figure out how many there are in our neighbourhood beyond a vague "hundreds."

A handful of grey squirrels was introduced to England in the nineteenth century, some say to amuse rich Victorians, and a few more immigrated to Scotland early in the twentieth century. Before long they were displacing the native red squirrels. The greys (which can sometimes be black or have red bits, as the ones in our neighbourhood do) have an advantage over the reds because they're bigger and their digestive systems allow them to eat seeds and nuts while they're unripe, so they deplete food sources before the red squirrels can use them. Greys breed twice a year instead of the reds' once, an obvious advantage in numbers. Worse yet, the greys are carriers of the dreaded squirrel poxvirus, which is lethal to the reds but doesn't affect the greys.

Conservationists fear the little red squirrel will become extinct in a decade. It's a serious situation and it sounds like war, although the Brits, being Brits, manage to have a little fun with it. One official suggested a good control would be to put squirrels on the nation's dinner plates—squirrel casserole, squirrel roasted and smoked, squirrel pâté, squirrel burgers (which he, having sampled, pronounced delicious). A hotel restaurant in Cumbria, England, makes little squirrel pancakes and serves them as canapés; they're made from rodents trapped on the hotel's large woodland. "They taste rather nice, a bit like rabbit," the manager was quoted as saying in a newspaper story. Come to think of it, Catharine Parr Traill, who endured many privations as a Canadian pioneer in the early 1800s and probably ate things she never dreamed she would, described the meat of roast squirrel as "tender, white and delicate, like that of a young rabbit," in *Canadian Crusoes*. However, she also turned squirrels into a humanlike family in her children's book, *Lady Mary and Her Nurse*. And think of the movies and other children's books with squirrels as well as raccoons as their heroes!

The grey invaders are not only reducing the population of the beloved native red squirrel, but they're also dining on the bark of maples, pines, and hemlocks in winter, when other food is less available, leaving the trees vulnerable to disease. According to England's Confederation of Forest Industries, squirrel damage costs the industry ten million pounds a year.

So this is serious stuff, much more than damage to a few birdfeeders in my backyard or the loss of a dozen or so tulips and a pair or two of pantyhose. It's a good reason not to import alien and invasive species—like the few starlings brought to New York more than a century ago to satisfy someone's longing for the birds of home. They too have proliferated and now call every part of this continent home. The same goes for the gypsy moth, a burgeoning problem where I live—it was brought to Massachusetts in 1869 with the expectation that its larvae would spin silk as fine as its Asian cousins did and start a whole new and vastly profitable industry here. They didn't. But they knew how to multiply, and they now defoliate close to a million forested acres *each year* in the U.S. and are eating their way north. Spraying programs using the biological control *Bacillus thuringiensis,* a natural soil-dwelling bacterium used as a pesticide, during the days the larvae are in evidence have been in effect for a couple of years in my community; so far we don't know what effect they've actually had.

Measures stronger than turning the grey squirrel into a gaming delicacy are being considered to deal with its spread in the U.K., including contraceptives and planting more conifers so that the red squirrels will have more of the food they're able to eat. By early 2008 close to twelve thousand squirrels, estimated to be two-thirds of the local population, had been culled in Northumberland, Scotland, by the Red Squirrel Protection Partnership, using what was referred to as humane pest control, which could be poisoning with the drug warfarin or shooting. The local environmental department advises that a humane way to shoot them is to gather the squirrels in a cage before using your gun, I guess so that the squirrels have the emotional support of their buddies as they face the executioner. It's also suggested the squirrels could be lured into a sack and dispatched cranially with at least two firm blows of a hammer to each head. Drowning or gassing, however, is prohibited by the Wild Mammals Protection Act of 1996.

A landowner in Scotland has offered a bounty of ten pounds for every dead squirrel shot on his estate. "These aliens have to be eliminated," his groundskeeper said, according to a story in the *London Daily Telegraph*. Bounties aren't new—from 1932 to '57 (with the exception of the war years), Britain's ministry of agriculture paid from six to twelve pence for every grey tail brought into their offices, but the program didn't do much good—the squirrel population increased during that period.

We have red squirrels in Canada, although not in my neighbourhood. They're not the same breed as the *Sciurus vulgaris* native to Europe. North American red squirrels (*Tamiasciurus hudsonicus*, so named because they were first catalogued near Hudson Bay, in 1771), are sometimes known as pine squirrels because they dine on the cones available in coniferous forests, where they hang out. Another family, *T. douglasii*, is exclusive to British Columbia's Pacific coast (red squirrels are very territorial, unlike greys, which are a little more accepting of their brothers and sisters). Many subspecies of red squirrels have been identified, and those who study them say the genus can be divided into five major lineages, including flying squirrels. The eastern and western grey squirrels, although apparently more fecund, form a smaller branch of the family, with roughly three subspecies.

Who'd have thought my common backyard companion would have such an interesting family tree!

I'VE NOT HAD as much consort with the resident raccoons as I've had with the squirrels, for a couple of good reasons. First, although there are quite enough of them, thank you, there aren't as many raccoons as squirrels, and, second, they're nocturnal. My personal brushes with them tend to be limited to dealing with their 2 AM gruntings on the roof outside our bedroom window. *You can't do that on* my *house, you lascivious little beasts!* Even a pitcher or two of water thrown right on them from the window doesn't deter them.

The raccoons bother Chris beyond simple sleep interruption. He's in charge of our two small ponds, and although raccoons may not like a skinny dip they do like to fish in the moonlight. Too often I hear moans of frustration from the garden when Chris is on his morning pond inspection, and I know the raccoons have trashed the water lilies or the water hyacinths yet again. Like the squirrels, they don't eat the whole plant; they prefer to drag the plants out of the pond, sample the best parts of several and leave the rest to die. I swear they go after the vegetation because the fish won't co-operate—except for one dullard, the fish have so far escaped becoming a raccoon breakfast. They're wily enough to hide under the waterfall or an edging rock and escape those cunning little hands. Those cunning little hands! Even after we covered the openings on our garden lights with rigid wire mesh to keep little fingers out, they were able to pry the mesh off and pop out the bulbs.

I can probably count on two hands the number of raccoons in our neighbourhood, but inch for inch they're far more destructive than two hundred squirrels. I admit their little masked faces and waddling walk are kind of cute, especially on the kits, and raccoons *en famille* look awfully sweet staring down from the crook of the Norway maple as we have a candlelit dinner on the deck. Curious, smart, and resourceful, too... if they grew opposable thumbs the world would soon be theirs.

But we had to convince them that our garden wasn't the place to start on a quest for world domination. We tried rodent repellant sprayed around the pond, then sprinkled cayenne pepper and fenugreek seeds around it until the place began to smell like an Indian buffet. We tried socks filled with mothballs and ammonia-soaked rags. We sprayed the rocks around the pond with diluted ammonia and then began to worry about the fish. We tried a neighbour's remedy: a radio tuned loudly to an all-night talk show. It had successfully sent a mother and babies living in her garage fleeing—unfortunately to our next-door neighbour's shed, where they took up residence till the babies became adults. Our radio made me wonder who was having a party in our backyard when it woke me up in the middle of the night, and I feared another glare from the man over the fence, for which I wouldn't have blamed him. So we gave that up after a couple of nights. It didn't help anyway.

The second-last thing we tried was pantyhose filled with human hair. Chris was sure this would work because it came highly recommended to him by a ponding friend. So even thought it was high summer and the weather was scorching, I agreed to wear a couple of old pairs of pantyhose for a day to impart a human scent, and he asked the local hairdresser to save him her floor sweepings for a week. We cut the legs off the pantyhose, filled each with hair, tied the ends and laid the resulting sausages around the pond.

The next morning—no evidence of raccoon visits. Could this be the answer? But the following morning the hair sausages had been carefully placed in a row on the path several feet from the pond, and the water hyacinths were in shreds.

Our last, and successful, try was the rodent scarer, a nifty little gadget that hooks up to the hose and goes into action with a strong blast of water at the first sign of movement. I smile contentedly to myself when I hear its oscillating *chugga-chugga-*

shhoo in the middle of the night, but that's not too often anymore because the little beasts have learned to give it, and the pond, a wide berth.

I did have one memorable close encounter with a raccoon in my bathroom. This little fellow had persistently plagued us with nocturnal visits for two nights, convinced, it seemed, that it was our long-lost child. One night it broke in through main-floor screens three times and was successfully broomed out the front door each time; the next night it broke in a fourth time, made it to the basement, and crawled into the space between the floors. Getting rid of it on that visit had required several hundred dollars and the services of a pest-control company with a live trap and a can of tuna. Once the raccoon had been caught, we followed the instructions of the proprietor and took the rodent to the farthest corner of the backyard. Then we released it.

It didn't seem far enough away to us, and it wasn't.

About three o'clock in the wee hours of the third night, I arose as usual for a bathroom visit. I sat in the darkness so that I disturbed no one, as is my practice, and as my eyes became accustomed to the gloom I noticed a dark mound in the bathtub. I turned the light on. *Gasp!* Our friend the raccoon stared back at me, calmly nibbling on a pumice stone. How had it broken in and climbed the stairs without waking us?

I closed the door and, surprisingly calm, notified Chris. Dealing with an animal invader is man's work. Armed with his trusty broom and standing on the toilet, he tried to battle the beast out of the bathtub, into the hallway and down the stairs. No go. Good sense finally prevailed, and he opened the bathroom window, removed the screen, left the room, and closed the door. By morning the creature had returned to the wild.

But not for long. As we were having coffee and congratulating ourselves on one more victory, there was a ripping sound from the kitchen. We raced in: the raccoon was spread-eagled over what was left of the back-door screen, looking a little shocked itself.

Chris decided to fight fire with water. He grabbed the hose and gave the terrorist a good blast. For reasons we can't explain, the creature never attempted to break in again.

Such tales of bothersome raccoons seem to bolster the notion that there's no good to be had from their presence, but raccoons have had some proven value to humans over the years. An image of a raccoon carved on a conch shell, with its unmistakable masked face and ringed tail, was discovered in the Spiro archeological mounds in eastern Oklahoma. The site dates back thousands of years, to the pre-Columbian age, and was a centre of a large trading network that did business in obsidian, copper, shells, flint, and mica from all parts of the continent. It was also the home of leaders and a burial site, and the intricate designs on the conch shells are thought to have profound significance.

Could raccoons have been worshipped as rodent gods? More likely they were an important source of fur or food, which they still are today in some parts, particularly in the southern United States. Raccoon fur was fashionable in Canada during the middle of the twentieth century—I remember burying my face in the long fur of my mom's raccoon coat when I was a little girl and we'd go on Sunday car rides in our old Chevy, and I still have a picture of her standing in front of our house in Winnipeg, wearing the coat and her lace-up fur-trimmed galoshes.

Because raccoon fur was valuable, raising imported North American raccoons on farms was big business in Germany in the 1920s. In 1934, Herman Göring himself (he was then head of forestry for the Third Reich) allowed a pair of the animals to be released into the wild near Frankfurt to enrich the field for local hunters. More were accidentally liberated from a raccoon farm during Allied bombings in the Second World War, and the raccoons have been marching through Europe ever since—nearly a million are estimated to have invaded cities in Germany, much like the grey squirrels have done in the U.K. And just as they do at home, the expat raccoons are breaking into attics, feasting on insulation, ripping up lawns in a search of grubs and opening garbage cans with their nimble little fingers.

What we need to do is acquire a taste for raccoon meat, just like early settlers to this continent did, out of necessity no doubt. In a quest to see how one might cook it, I Googled "raccoon recipes" and came up with thousands. One site offered twenty-seven tasty preparations, among them sweet and sour raccoon, corn-fried raccoon (soaked in milk and coated in corn flakes), slow-cooker raccoon (with honey, sherry, and soy sauce— "tender and delicious!"), raccoon patties (with red currant sauce), raccoon tails (fooled ya—really a long cookie iced with stripes of melted chocolate), and stuffed roast raccoon (done like turkey and served with sweet potatoes and a choice of pickled beets or sweet and sour red cabbage). Sweet potatoes and strong spices like allspice or curry, and fruity accompaniments such as apples and pears, are popular complements to raccoon meat. All the recipes emphasize that most of the fat and all the musk or scent glands under the arms and legs must be removed or they will impart an unpleasant flavour or smell while cooking. But none tells you how to do it, or how to skin and prepare the beast.

I can't imagine my bathtub raccoon on a platter surrounded by sweet potatoes. If I were roughing it in the bush, as Catharine Parr Trail and her sister Susanna Moodie did, I might be able to, but garden acquaintances are not on my menu. And it's not just that I'm unfamiliar with the taste—perhaps they've taken on some kind of personae because they've lived in my backyard. But I've eaten cows and lambs although I've seen them gamboling on my uncles' farms, and I've eaten chicken after I've watched its head cut off, so why not squirrels and raccoons? I guess the short answer is that I'm just not hungry enough, but if I thought about it long enough I'd probably become a vegetarian.

SOME MAY QUIBBLE that cats don't qualify as wildlife, but we have lots of them in the neighbourhood and they're entirely welcome in our garden. Some people don't like cats at all, and others tolerate them, but never in a garden. Cats get blamed for every bird death and all the yellowing foliage at the bottom of hedges, even when they're innocent. Of course they aren't innocent all the time, I know. Any patch of soil may be considered a litter box, and although we're grateful for their fastidious habit of covering up the evidence, sometimes cats uproot plants in the process.

The man who formerly lived next door used to swear at our cats and throw stones at them when he thought I wasn't looking—once he even asked me why I didn't train them not to hunt birds. "Mice are okay," he growled. "We could do with less of those."

Few of my neighbours are so unrealistic. In fact, I'd say we live in a cat's paradise, and that's not counting the bowls of food my next-door neighbour Mary leaves out for felines that feel a bit peckish before mommy comes home. Within a radius of about six houses we have a baker's dozen of cats, and they coexist beautifully. They sun themselves together on one another's decks and frequently visit each other's place for a nap or a snack. Their friends' mommies and daddies accept this as a natural practice, even though cats are usually thought of as aloof, self-sufficient creatures.

In our neighbourhood, we know that's not so. Our cats may not provide the best vermin control, but they're sociable creatures, and over the years they've enhanced the spirit of the place.

159

Federico Fellini, better known as Fred, a handsome fellow with yellow eyes and a swishy tail who lives next door, used to come by at least twice a day to see our little calico Madame Mao, but she's sadly gone now. He's also older and beginning to look like a fading roué; now he drops by only once a day in summer for old times' sake. We don't see Otis anymore, but we remember him fondly; he was a blindingly beautiful ginger male whose IQ didn't measure up to his looks. He'd come by every night for a little supper, but he was tragically killed by a fox, which taught us all to keep our cats indoors at night. Benny and Jenny, two Maine coon cats who now live at Otis's house, are always around, but although Benny is welcome to visit our deck he's been banished from coming inside because he likes to mark his territory. He was the talk of the neighbourhood when he got his recent poodle cut: it's the latest cut for furry cats, with ruffs around the neck and feet and the end of the tail, but his was done out of necessity. His long coat had become so tangled he had to have most of it shaved off. He looked like a circus lion and was shunned by the other cats for a few weeks.

Rusty and Lily, a brother and sister who live on the other side of us, are so long and lithe they must have some Siamese blood; they love to explore our garden or doze under a shrub. Shamus McGinty has always been a little bit feisty, but as an older cat he's become downright aggressive, so we've had to discourage him from visiting. This is a first—the felines who live around here generally have perfect manners.

Our own cats—we've had nine all told, three at present—have always considered our garden their personal jungle, and they allow us in it for the purposes of upkeep only. Whenever we walk out to make a compost deposit, one of them has always appeared from nowhere and accompanied us down the path. They've never been very helpful at chasing away squirrels; for that I expect you need a dog. The cats treat squirrels as play-things, but with respect: they creep up on them and pause, hind ends waggling, then race towards them like mad, veering off at the last minute because they really don't want to tangle with those claws and teeth. The squirrels stare back insolently, still nibbling. Raccoons are generally ignored, but skunks can be fun. I've actually seen the gregarious Benny gamboling with a black and white juvenile on the lawn across the street, and other neighbours have reported similar sightings. So far, no disasters.

All the neighbourhood cats love Chris for the pond he built. The fish are an endless fascination and worth a paw jab or two, but as fishers the cats have thankfully been useless. I expect they're too well fed and are just answering some dim call of nature. The compost bin provides the most diversion. Why, a cat can spend all day waiting for a mouse to emerge, and when one does the excitement knows no bounds.

Doug, one of our cats from a few years back, had severe agoraphobia and other neurotic disorders and was never able to enjoy the outdoors. I had a soft spot for her (she was named after the illusionist Doug Henning because she was always doing a disappearing act) because of my own earlier affliction, and I tried to introduce her slowly to the magic of the world outside but she would have none of it. She lived to be twenty years old, and I think she achieved some kind of happiness in her old age, once her hearing and sight diminished. The sounds of the wind and the presence of strange cats on our deck no longer threat-ened her, and she'd sometimes spend hours out there in the sun.

161

Madame Mao, a.k.a. Norma Desmond, a darling, tiny cal-ico, is my all-time favourite. She died in my arms a couple of years ago at eighteen, gazing tiredly into my eyes as I wept copi-ously and promised her we'd meet again someday. Mao became known as Norma because of her love for cameras, a predilection that became blatantly obvious once we started to do the television show intros and extros in our garden. Every time we were ready to shoot, Mao would saunter onto the set. "Yes, Mr. De-Mille, I'm ready for my close-up," I could almost hear her say, and she'd step in front of me, throwing a seductive glance at the director. Of course there'd be a little *maow*, too, just to let everyone know she was the real star here and ready to do everything she could to make the scene work, and a little glance upward at my co-host Kevin as she wound around his ankles. Then a nice rub of her nose on his hand as he bent to pet her. Oh, I've seen it all, the little scene stealer. The crew soon caught on to her tactics, but she was so smart and adorable she was allowed to stay. She even made the final cut of a few episodes and appeared nationally, although she never got a credit for her cameos.

I will never forget Mao, but we still have her sister Radar, a now twenty-one-year-old fragile and possibly overmedicated geriatric who remains well loved despite her frequent accidents and pilling times. And we've fallen in love with two new males, the tabby brothers Rufus and Eli. They're plump and slim, respectively: Rufus is an easygoing comfort lover with a kitten's mew that doesn't suit his significant size, and the quick, bright Eli we're sure has a feline version of attention deficit disorder. They're the best hunters yet and have brought home many dead mice for us to admire. Unfortunately, a few birds have met their deaths in Eli's jaws, too; we have to keep a closer watch over him. But he's young and may soon settle into the neighbourhood non-aggression policy.

I always thought that Egyptian pharaohs were the first people to adore cats, but I read recently that a feline was found buried next to its owner and many valuables in a 9,500-year-old tomb in Cyprus. This was the neolithic period and predates the Egyptians by about four thousand years. I also read recently about cats in the future, in Margaret Atwood's novel *Oryx and Crake*. Atwood describe how the humanoid People of Crake attempt to cure Snowman, the protagonist, of an infected foot by gathering around him and purring. This feline therapy had been bred into the Crake people because of its curative powers, to which any cat owner who's sat with a purring cat on his or her lap will attest.

Cats purr when they're content but also when they're injured, frightened, or giving birth, a fact that suggests purring is also a survival mechanism. If you connect this to research showing that vibrational stimulation helps 82 per cent of people suffering acute pain and also generates the growth of new tissue, improves circulation, reduces swelling and inhibits bacterial growth, doesn't it make you ask whether perhaps our felines know something we don't?

CHAPTER 12

The

ITALIAN CONNECTION

. . . . .

URING MY BUSY years with the magazine and the television show, I didn't have time to consider making major changes to the garden. Besides, I was reasonably content with the way it looked—with its style, in any case. It was a typical cottage garden, the loose, blowsy English kind I'd been nurtured in, and although it could get out of hand now and again, it was my garden and it was second nature to me.

Then along came another opportunity to learn from, in the form of a 1999 tour of the more formal classical gardens of Tuscany and Rome, organized by a travel company and *Canadian Gardening* magazine. That tour shifted my perspective and opened my eyes.

The tour focused on historical gardens, but, because this was Italy, architecture, history, and good food were intrinsic elements. Luckily for me, I was elected to tag along as the tour host and representative of the magazine. Also luckily for me, although he gave a little eye roll at the thought of visiting all those gardens, the intrinsic elements allowed me to persuade Chris that he ought to play consort.

Although I'd hosted a smaller tour of twelve people up the coast of California in '97 with the same tour company and *Canadian Gardening*, neither Chris nor I was accustomed to travelling with a large group of people (there were twenty-six of us), or to answering 8:30 AM hotel lobby calls to board the bus for the next garden tour. On our personal vacations we'd learned the value of exploring a cathedral or Mayan ruin on our own, guidebook in hand, and of sightseeing leisurely, working in plenty of café stops and piazza sits to watch the world go by. It seemed to us that soaking up as much local colour as we could in a relaxed way was the best way to learn something about the customs and culture of another country.

We were apprehensive about the size of the group, but we need not have worried. Except for one difficult soul, who actually had the effect of bonding the rest of us together, our group proved to be fellow travellers who shared many interests, if not all of them all the time. A few, including the surgeon who precision-plants his perennials I mentioned earlier, we continue to see.

Most of the gardens we toured were created during the Renaissance, that flowering of culture and thought that grew out of the Middle Ages; some had their origins in the eleventh or twelfth centuries, although most had changed considerably over the years through human or nature's hands. I'd helped research and choose the gardens, but I wasn't familiar with them except through books and photographs, and I was as anxious as anyone to see them.

We started in Florence, the city with a postcard view on every corner, but by the end of the first day I was wondering where all the flowers were. Clipped greenery and good "bones" were clearly more important. I was disappointed and a little concerned that my touring companions might not feel they were getting their money's worth. Of course, we saw a few flowers—in the narrow courtyard garden of the Giardino Budini Gattai, the first garden we visited, containers spilling over with bright bougainvillea were displayed. But that was it for this *giardino*—simple, straightforward design was its strong point.

The backbone of the garden at Budini Gattai, a sixteenth-century palace in the middle of Florence now owned by a banking family and used as offices, was a pebble-mosaic pathway that marked the long axis of the garden, with a crossing path that divided the area into squares. The original family's emblem, laid out in black slate and gold stones, was worked into the mosaic square at the intersection. Lovely, but... I stood on the long arm of the path looking towards the end of the garden, where an arched doorway filled with golden light beckoned me. *It's like a light at the end of the tunnel,* I suddenly thought. I had this thought more than once on this trip, looking down a long pathway or avenue with a tantalizing destination or focal point in the distance. Straight lines have never appealed to me, but these had a certain mathematical precision, with a lovely payoff gracing the end of the view.

The monumental Boboli Gardens, started in 1549 behind their home, the Pitti Palace, by the Medici Duke Cosimo I for his wife, Eleonora, was almost entirely flower free and daunting in its size and formal design. We spent the afternoon of that first day at the Boboli prowling up and down grassy terraces and wide gravel pathways lined with centuries-old cypress, checking out the classical statues above concentric rows of seating in the curved stone amphitheatre (where performances are still occasionally staged), exploring the woods or the cool grottoes. We gasped to hear the age of the Egyptian obelisk in the centre of the amphitheatre (commissioned by Ramses II in 1200

BC and brought to Italy in the fifteenth century by the Medicis) and admired the view of Florence from the top of the Boboli hill. We discovered Madama's secret garden, a smallish plot of clipped greenery with a medieval flavour, tucked away behind a wall near the palace.

But except for the old roses and pots of citrus on a small island in the centre of a large oval pond, and a formal rose garden at the top of the hill, there was not a bloom to be seen. The Boboli was too big and too green—eleven acres big, spreading out well to the right behind the palace—and I couldn't make head nor tail of the vast expanses of grass and paving. Did people really garden this way five hundred years ago? Were we trying to take in too much in one day?

By the end of the afternoon, with my muscles and my brain tired and my knee complaining, I sank onto the steps at the back of the Pitti Palace, gazing straight ahead at the amphitheatre, which faces the palace and lines up with the exact centre of its façade. And here I experienced a mini-revelation. The view was austere, perhaps, but definitely symmetrical and oddly pleasing in a calming sort of way. The stone arms of the amphitheatre's seating, shaped like a horseshoe, reached out to me. The twenty-four curved niches above the seats, containing graceful statues depicting ancient myths, were stationed evenly around the curve. Dead in the centre of the view, poking its pointy head above the horizon and bisecting the path behind it that was taking more visitors uphill to the view of Florence, was the Egyptian obelisk. It was a marvel of formal balance.

I began to admire the Boboli's hedges. Tall and dense, they were clipped with precision, some with alcoves cut into them to hold statues or benches, some merging into each other in perfect symmetry. *Like green walls*, I thought. *Walls that protect and define the space.*

The Boboli is a park more than a garden, but it started out as a more intimate space. In the beginning, Eleonora's garden was made up only of the part of the Boboli I could see from where I was sitting on the steps of the Pitti Palace: the amphitheatre, which had been carved out of the hill and was originally formed with hedges and greenery, and the long hill behind it, terraced and planted with tall oaks, shiny bay laurel and mounding viburnum bushes. Over the next few centuries the Boboli was more than doubled in size by subsequent Medicis and other rulers of Florence, and added to and subtracted from it were such embellishments as labyrinths, an aviary, and a menagerie, plus dozens of pieces of sculpture. Today a bird would have a better appreciation of the overall plan than a human being sitting on the steps of the Uffizi. I rather wished I could have seen it in its original, simpler form.

Flowers made a slightly more emphatic appearance in the garden of the Villa Medici in Fiesole, a pretty hilltop village with an incomparable view of the tile roofs of Florence. The musical chiming of church bells marking the hour floated up to the garden as we strolled along the raised wisteria-covered carriageway from the gatehouse to the villa. Below us to our left stretched a large quartered garden; each quarter was edged with low, clipped boxwood and filled with bright orange marigolds. Potted lemon trees marked the corners and were stationed along the front of the *limonaia*—a graceful, low building with arched doorways where the lemon trees were stored over winter. It had been converted into apartments. *For whom?* I wondered. *Could I rent one?* We descended the garden stairs to the sunken garden carved out of the hillside. I bent down to examine the marigolds. They were Crackerjack I was certain, my old favourite, but they looked loud and vulgar in this serene and otherwise green garden.

This section of the villa's garden had probably contained vegetables in the days of the garden's youth in the mid-1400s, we were told by our guide, and the villa was what you might describe as transitional during its time, meaning it bridged the years between the Middle Ages and the Renaissance. People had not yet become accustomed to living freely outside village walls, which had protected them from invaders and pillagers during more uncertain times. Even medieval farmers lived inside their villages, she said, and journeyed out every morning to cultivate their crops in the fields. This villa was an innovation for its time: it was built outside the walls of the village but on a nearly inaccessible slope so that interlopers could not easily approach and was erected at great cost and with much engineering skill. It became a landmark, and the protected sunny garden in the side of the hill had an unexpected virtue: a microclimate that allowed the cultivation of exotic and tender plants.

The villa's history was at least as fascinating as the garden's: the villa had been built for Giovanni de Medici, a favourite son of Cosimo de Medici, an influential Florentine banker who carried considerable political sway in the community. Giovanni was a lustful, overweight man who loved music, art, and beauty; unfortunately he died young, no doubt as a result of his indulgences, and the villa was inherited by Lorenzo the Magnificent, a grandson of Cosimo and nephew of Giovanni, and a politician and diplomat. Lorenzo's overwrought title was simply a mark of respect for a person of his stature, said the guide—it didn't mean he was royalty—but Lorenzo lived up to the sobriquet: he was a cultured man who supported scholars and the arts with his wealth, notably such giants as Leonardo da Vinci and Michelangelo. Lorenzo too died young—at forty-three, and only six months before Christopher Columbus crossed the Atlantic and discovered a new continent. It was reported that the local church steeple was struck by lightning at the moment of his death, and Florentines were so moved by his early demise that the entire population attended his funeral.

Details like this fired my imagination.

I could see a carriage *clip-clopp*ing its way under the wisteria'd pergola towards the villa, carrying Leonardo or Michelangelo to a small supper to arrange funding for a painting or a sculpture. (The only wrinkle in this little scenario was that the carriageway was built a couple centuries after Lorenzo's death, but I didn't learn that till later.) I could see a gathering of the cognoscenti on the terrace overlooking Florence, discussing a new church fresco or a piazza statue. I could see a fifteenth-century gardener in old grey overalls and straw hat, a man not unlike Uncle Ren, working in the warm sun in that beautiful four-square garden to pick the sweet, juicy tomatoes so particular to Italy, or clipping lavender for the pillow of Giovanni's latest conquest. *Oh stop it*, I thought. *It probably never happened this way at all.*

But I realized I was hooked. Even if the style of these gardens, and the others I was about to see, weren't exactly my taste, there was history here—real people building villas and making gardens centuries ago, following prevailing customs and styles. Plants may die and garden walls may crumble, but human nature doesn't change much. The people who designed and tended these gardens were probably much like me or you, although richer and more powerful, and I was starting to feel curious about their lives and how they made their gardens.

I didn't feel the strong presence of former owners at Villa Gamberaia, which lies east of Fiesole near the village of Settignano, perhaps because the garden and its beautiful, classic plan commanded my attention. Like Villa Medici, Gamberaia has a breathtaking view of olive groves and gentle hills rolling down to the glimmering Arno River and Florence in the distance. It's large compared with contemporary suburban gardens like mine but on the small side for a Renaissance garden, and its beautifully proportioned geometrics, its changes of levels and separate areas enclosed by hedges and balustrades, give it a spacious yet intimate feeling. It's easy to read, as garden designers and artists might say.

Rows of cypress lining the entrance road to the creamy stucco villa speak of all the pictures you've ever seen of Tuscan hillside villas, this one with not a hint of crumbling walls despite its age. It was built in the fifteenth century, then enlarged in the seventeenth by the family that created the original garden, and generations of owners have maintained and improved the garden without modifying the original plan. *I can't imagine future owners preserving my garden,* I thought to myself. *Mine will probably be turned into townhouses.* The Villa Gamberaia garden is structured on the same straight-from-the-house axis as the amphitheatre of the Boboli Gardens, subdivided by cross-paths that define the spaces. We took in the plan from the back of the villa, our guide telling us that this was the basic grid that underlay the design of most Renaissance gardens, then we began to explore: first the four rectangular pools, each framed with clipped boxwood. These once made up a large four-square rose garden, but in the late nineteenth century the beds were turned into still pools that reflect the sky. Farther back, a curved lily pond is bordered by low hedges clipped to rise like ziggurats, and a tall semicircular cypress hedge cut with arched openings offers framed views of the valley below. A bowling green beside the villa is a long expanse of perfect grass with pots of citrus arranged down its centre, and beside it is a hidden garden, dim and cool and heavily planted with trees that make it truly mysterious. The hidden garden leads to a grotto, reached via stone steps, with pebbles and shells embedded in its walls and niches.

Villa Gamberaia's *limonaia*, beyond a fragrant herb garden, has also been converted to apartments, and we toured them, too. This time I voiced my silent question—*Can I rent one?* Yes, they're available for vacation rentals, as are the rooms in the main villa, lovely high-ceilinged places with elegant furnishings. We checked them out, too, knowing full well we could never afford them.

Over the following week our bus rumbled through Tuscany on its way to Rome, stopping at this garden and that to view more gorgeous historic clipped hedges, ancient walls, marble statuaries, balustrades, secret gardens, and reflecting pools. I began to fear the onset of Stendahl syndrome, and I could see by the looks on my fellow travellers' faces that I was not alone. Our developing camaraderie over the meals we shared helped balance the cycle of gardens, and afternoon surprises, like the pots of delicious wild boar pâté accompanied by chewy, crusty Tuscan bread and cold white wine we shared in one of the gardens, became memorable occasions. But the highlight of the trip, one we still talk about, was the Big Lunch.

It was planned as a cooking demonstration in the *limonaia* at Villa Bernardini in Lucca after a tour of the villa's garden, to be followed by a light lunch featuring the appetizers the chef had shown us how to prepare. After all the four-course lunches we'd been having, we thought this was a capital idea, especially knowing that a gala prime rib dinner for the whole party was on the hotel menu that evening. We savoured the bruschetta, crostini with red pepper sauce, and sausage wrapped in pecorino cheese and drank the wine, and we were starting to gather up our sun hats and bags when the chef entered, beaming, with what looked like a small casket on a tray. It was his specialty, *lardo di colonnato.* The guide explained that yes, it was indeed lard, but a special kind, marinated in herbs and aged in a marble cask for a month in a cave. We were too polite to say no (too *Canadian*, said Chris), so down it went. Delicious, too, in a high-cholesterol kind of way. More wine was poured. Then the chef brought out eggplant with mint and a bread-and-tomato salad, and steaming platters of pasta shaped like clouds with tomato sauce. Wine was poured again. At three o'clock we were digging into pork with roasted vegetables. At three-thirty, Tuscan apple pie.

There were ten courses in all. We rolled back onto the bus, pleading with the tour guide to cancel our gala hotel dinner; we were simply too full, swearing we'd never eat again, but hadn't it been fun! Three hours later, eighteen of the twenty-six turned up for the roast beef. Didn't I tell you that gardeners like to eat?

OF COURSE I didn't succumb to Stendahl, and I absorbed as many highlights as I could on the hour-or-two visits to the gardens. I did see flowers, but they were handled more subtly than in our gardens at home—a discreet display of roses, for example. Iris and lavender grew casually with grey-green santolina at Villa Gamberaia, but flower beds were generally formal—carpets of one kind and colour of annual tucked inside low boxwood hedges, as with the marigolds in the rectangular beds at the Villa Medici; I also saw round and triangular beds of annual blue ageratum or dwarf yellow zinnias. These garden-variety annuals made a strong statement when planted in one dense mass. Like the long, straight pathways, the *allées* of trees impressed me, especially when they were clipped to a definitive shape and guided one's eye to the villa's entrance or a fountain or gazebo, or even to a huge branching tree at the far end.

Water was present in every garden, in reflecting pools, grottoes, nymphaea, cascades, jets, or *giochi d'acqua*, which translates as a water joke or game. In the middle years of the Renaissance

173

these would squirt water up a lady's petticoat or on a gentleman's pants if they stepped on the wrong stone walking over a path. *Doesn't seem very funny to me,* I thought. *Some kind of Renaissance mean streak?* Our guide said it was all in good fun, no harm meant, nearly every garden had one—in fact, we were going to see one of the best *giochi d'acqua* that very afternoon. It was still in operating order, although never used in case it became damaged. This one delivered a triple whammy: guests would trigger a strong spray as they took an after-dinner promenade along the balcony overlooking the garden; I could see them shrieking down the stairs, only to be sprayed again from the beds on each side as they raced along the lower path to the safety of the grotto at the end of the garden, where—guess what?—another dousing greeted them, this time a good drenching from above. I think I might have turned down the next invitation to dine.

Every castle or villa had a secret garden, most so hidden you would never notice them unless pointed in their direction by the guide. At the Castello Ruspoli in the Lazio village of Vignanello, the secret garden clung to a narrow terrace below the castle walls and was reached through a hidden staircase within the walls. It's probably four hundred years old and is being meticulously restored and planted with old garden roses by the present owner (with grants from the European Union and Casa di Risparmio di Roma, which assists with the financing of many historic properties). At Lucca's Villa Reale, owned by Napoleon Bonaparte's sister Elisa Baciocchi in the early nineteenth century, you'd walk right by the secret garden unless you happened to notice an unobtrusive opening in the hedge or by chance glance down over a certain wall. But I guess that's the raison d'etre of a secret garden, isn't it?

It seemed a shame that Elisa's secret garden could so easily be missed: it was made up of a pattern of intricate scrolls and circles made of clipped green- and yellow-foliaged evergreens (I tried to find out the name of the the yellow variety, but no one knew), with the spaces inside the foliage scrolls and circles filled with crushed red tile and black stones instead of flowers.

I couldn't decide whether Elisa was a woman almost as ambitious as her brother or a generous ruler with the good of her people at heart. She bought the Villa Reale, also known as Villa Marlia and dating back to about 1650, when she was made Princess of Lucca (later Sovereign of all of Tuscany) in the early 1800s, no doubt by you-know-who. The gardens already had many attributes, including a famous semicircular green theatre with a high backdrop of clipped yew and alcoves holding lovely—and still-standing—marble statues of Columbine, Pantalone, and Balanzone. It was planted in 1642 and is still green and healthy, although I can't imagine with the original yew. Paganini played his violin here and is said to have rendered the music so beautifully he reduced Elisa to tears and swoons, which made her resolve to turn her property into a park for the people. Or perhaps for herself. So she began buying up the neighbours' properties, including the local bishop's summer palace next door, and remodelling the gardens in Empire style, her own taste. When Napoleon's empire fell a few years later, Elisa was gone, thankfully before she could destroy all the historical features of the property.

Villa Reale passed into the hands of a few dukes and was eventually taken over by Victor Emmanuel II, who gave it to Prince Charles of Capua; the nearly penniless Charles had been disinherited because he married a commoner, an Englishwoman. They had a son (also Prince Charles but known to most people as "the mad prince") who liked to gamble, and the property had to be sold to pay his debts. By this time, can you believe it, it was 1918! Since then Villa Reale has been in the same family, which has completed extensive restorations and has opened the park to guided tours, just as Elisa intended.

Do you see how much history you can learn on a garden tour?

BUT IN THE END garden tours are garden tours, not classrooms or research libraries. My appetite was whetted by these stories our guides told about Renaissance gardens and their owners, and I was hungry for more. For satisfaction I had to hit the books.

One could read for days and never know all there is to know about how and why Renaissance gardens came to be. But the larger picture is that times were changing, and Renaissance gardens changed with them. The world was freeing itself of the restrictions of the Middle Ages; trade had revived, and returning merchants were bringing new ideas back to Italy. There was new interest in classical learning, including a look back to the philosophy and teachings of ancient Rome and to Greece, where gardens had been places of rest and philosophical exchange, as well as repositories of beautiful statues and architectural features. After the Renaissance dawned, gardens began to look outward again, beyond the walls of medieval times and into the countryside around them, just as the Medici villa at Fiesole had done.

But order was also important—order in music, art, architecture, and gardens that reflected the perfection of nature. Humanism dominated: nature may have had a grand design, but man was the microcosm of that design. Man could subdue nature and create his own vision of it, especially in the garden. Mathematical precision, proportion, and perspective became as important to gardens as they were to architecture and painting.

In the early Renaissance, the man who laid down the rules was Leon Battista Alberti, a person of many talents. He devoted one of the ten volumes of his treatise on architecture, *On the Art of Building* (*De Re Aedificatoria*) to the rules of gardening. (His book was first published in the fifteenth century and was reprinted several times into the eighteenth.) He proposed designs with "circles, semicircles and other geometric figures found in the field of building..." and "rows of trees set out in lines, with equal spacing between them and corresponding angles." Just like our friend the surgeon! A perfectly designed garden would have a central axis leading from the house, intersected by crossed axes so that it would become a series of smaller areas, which were often separated by pergolas or hedges, clipped topiaries and rows of trees. These areas might be connected to the house by terraces or long staircases, and the central axis would always culminate in a view—a structure, a fountain, or even a woodland.

Alberti is often referred to as the original Renaissance man. He studied law, became a priest and an adviser to Pope Nicholas v, was an accomplished cryptographer, and was skilled in Latin verse. He wrote several books that were considered breakthroughs, taking art and architecture beyond the gothic past, including *On Painting* (*De Pictura*), a scientific study of perspective in painting. He also wrote an autobiography (in the third person, a style of the time) in which he said he was capable of "standing with his feet together and springing over a man's head."

In *The Story of Gardening,* Penelope Hobhouse puts a little perspective on the man's many talents. She sniffs that while he claimed to simply adapt concepts from early Roman authors such as Cato, Virgil, and Pliny the Younger, much of the advice he gives is actually lifted word for word from their works.

The Renaissance garden went through several stages, from the early to the high, the baroque, the mannerist (during which all those water tricks were developed, plus other water features using complicated hydraulics for spectacular effects, such as you see at the Villa d'Este in Tivoli), and the neoclassic or romantic periods. This took four centuries, and anyone interested in anthropology or history will find it a fascinating period.

Despite her reservations about Alberti, Penelope Hobhouse was quite firm about one thing: the rules of the Renaissance garden are here to stay, even if we don't rigidly follow them. "Even designers who blanch at the idea of formality often use ways of organizing space in a garden that stems from the Renaissance, though they may disguise the geometry, right angles and axial lines by natural-looking, curvaceous planting," she wrote in *Gardening*.

And this, in fact, is true of my garden: its basic structure is a conjoining of circles and squares that form a grid over the space—the "curvilinear flow" referred to by my friend the designer—and they are subtly disguised by the soft lines of the garden beds. There are focal points, too: the arbour hiding the compost, on an axis straight from the French doors; the birdbath, a less-dominant focus on roughly the same axis, in the centre of the winding stepping-stone path through the main garden; even the bench under the Norway maple is a secondary focal point.

But my garden lacked the discipline I could see in the classical gardens, and I noticed this as soon as the taxi dropped us off at the foot of our driveway after our return from two glorious weeks eating and garden-visiting our way through Italy. My garden was messy. The front looked like a harlot dancing the can-can, her ample bosom falling over the top of her bodice. The back was more restrained, but the shapes needed definition.

So what did I do? I took a page out of Signor Alberti's *On the Art of Building* and planted a low hedge of clipped boxwood in a semicircle straight ahead of the French doors, a similar principle to Eleonora's green amphitheatre in the Boboli Gardens. It separates some low thymes from the taller perennials on the other side and defines a semicircle that's part of my friend's original design, which had formerly been invisible. In the front I added a delicate willow arch at the property line, where the narrow gravel path stopped dead at the neighbour's lawn. It provides another focal point and carries the eye under it to my neighbour's lawn and shrubs beyond.

Then I took out the secateurs. *Here, take that you undisciplined catmint! I'll get you under control, you wild aster!* They were small remedies, but they cured what ailed my garden.

❦

CHAPTER 13

Searching

FOR EVERYMAN'S GARDEN

. . . . .

IF THEY'RE DISCUSSED at all by garden historians and scholars, the gardens of people like you and me are often described as "vernacular." Mine was, once, and not by a historian or a scholar but by a garden designer I like a lot and whose work I respect a great deal. "Your garden is a really effective example of a vernacular type," she said as she wandered the path through the big backyard bed.

She didn't look as though she was delivering bad news, but I felt a little hurt. Was she implying my garden "worked" at some basic gardening level but that it was ordinary, that it didn't measure up to professional design standards? Maybe it struck her as a little vulgar, like common slang, which is how I'd heard the word used.

At this point in my garden's development I thought it looked pretty good, with the front a couple of seasons into its growth and the back well established after our house-and-garden renovation. I was generally pleased with it—as much as a gardener can be at a given moment, anyway—so I was rather taken aback by her comment and didn't ask what she meant. But I looked up the word later. Meaning number four in my dictionary said: "Characteristic of a specific locality or country; a vernacular art." Seeing that made me feel better. On further reading I found many garden scholars weighing in on the subject of vernacular gardens. They opined that a vernacular garden doesn't make a grand statement or have any notion of artistic endeavour. Nor does it exist as a work of art, as do great gardens of past centuries—famous ones like Louis xiv's Versailles, Cardinal Ippolito ii's palatial Villa d'Este in Tivoli, Italy, or the Alhambra, the beguiling Moorish palace and garden complex in Granada, Spain. Rather, the consensus was that a vernacular garden is a simple, local garden, containing the same kinds of plants as other gardens in the area and conforming generally to local styles.

In my opinion this definition, although true, is a little understated. I agree that vernacular gardens belong to ordinary people who may not have aspirations of grandeur, but they do have *some* aspirations: they aim to make gardens that are places of pleasure and repose, where they can grow veggies as well as flowers if they like, or just one or the other, places where they can dig and plant and meditate, and have alfresco suppers and wedding parties. (We've had two of the latter in our garden— our own and a lovely reception after the wedding of my son Joe and his wife, Chrissy.) Most gardeners also like to express themselves in their gardens with art and decoration, too—sometimes, I admit, with rather bizarre results. But gardens like these have a personal stamp, and so they diverge from the scholars' rather rigid definition of vernacular. I must have visited hundreds of ordinary people's gardens for *Canadian Gardening*, both the magazine and the tv show, and found each to be unique and obviously used as an opportunity for self-expression; one could never lump them together under one label. Almost invariably they disclosed something about the owners. I think that's probably a fair description of our garden, too.

I began to wonder whether ordinary people of the Renaissance or the Middle Ages had gardens described as vernacular. I found that although we know something about medieval monastery gardens because the monks kept records, little documentation exists about gardens beyond the monastery walls. Paintings abound of medieval romancing, showing feasting and flute playing in lovely gardens with arbours, topiaries, and turf seats, but it turns out these are mostly Flemish miniatures from the fifteenth century, and none can be validated as accurate because none are of known gardens. They could have sprung from someone's imagination, in other words. But it's nice to dream that this depiction is the way common folk enjoyed their gardens back then.

I could find nothing written about vernacular gardens during the Renaissance, either—judging by the available literature on the subject all gardens of that time occupied acres of land and were inspired by monocular perspective and designed with vistas, recessions, and avenues in mind. Ancient Rome is a different matter: we know that both utilitarian and decorative pleasure gardens were part of the daily life of ordinary citizens during that time, thanks to the ruins at Pompeii and Herculaneum, with their rich archeological records of outdoor living in courtyard gardens with fruit trees and *trompe l'oeil* paintings on the garden walls. Pliny the Younger also wrote often about his villa gardens at Laurentium and Tusculum, describing the pools, colonnades, and gardens planted with boxwood hedges, pergolas covered with grapevines, avenues of statuary and fruit trees.

But Pliny was no plebeian, so I suppose his gardens don't officially qualify as vernacular. But one must conclude the common folk of his time had to raise vegetables, even if that's all they had space for. Or perhaps they had community allotment gardens, with grapevines and flowers, where they met to socialize as they did at the public baths . . .

It's a shame there isn't more information around about the vernacular gardens of past centuries to give our imaginations something to go on, but apparently most of it didn't seem important enough to record, and scholars have never spent much time studying the subject anyway. They're more interested in the big picture. As Patrick Taylor writes in *The Oxford Companion to the Garden,* "A garden historian may travel a great distance to see, for example, Versailles, but will pay no attention to the front gardens in the street in which he lives." Pity.

Then again, anthropologists sometimes put the gardens of ordinary people under their microscopes because gardens reflect the culture of a civilization, and if you travel and don't wear blinkers you will soon notice this fact, especially if you can get yourself invited into someone's garden. In Mexico I've visited modest walled homes with one small door and one window showing to the street, in the Spanish tradition; inside, the main room opens to a central courtyard containing a small pool, a colourful tiled patio, and many exotic (to me, anyway) potted plants; these gardens are reminiscent of the peristyle gardens of Pompeii and Herculaneum. On a garden tour of Holland, I noticed front-yard gardens of several types—vegetable parterres outlined in low, clipped boxwood hedges and formal knot gardens sporting a graceful bench for an afternoon sit, to loosely styled perennial and shrub gardens; one such garden inspired my own front garden. On trips to southern California, where Joe and Chrissy now live, I've admired a few casual family-style backyards with Mediterranean plants, turquoise swimming pools, outdoor kitchens, and lots of big comfy couches and loungers—items hardly weather-worthy in my northern climate but typical of southern California's style. In Arizona I lusted after the minimalist southwestern gardens with huge saguaro cactus and mouse-eared prickly pear cactus planted in sand or gravel, plus brilliant purple and pink verbena and other drought-resistant perennial plants. In southern Italy, I envied edible back gardens with rows of luscious tomatoes and beans, an olive and a lemon tree, a pergola with grapes, an oven for making pizza and preparing tomatoes for the *cucina*, plus lots of family space. Many of the first-generation Portuguese and Italian residents who live in our Mississauga neighbourhood have brought their traditions with them and have similar vernacular gardens here, including outdoor ovens. I love the pergolas laden with grape-vines that take up a third of the backyard—and under which loud alfresco suppers sometimes take place—and the working sheds that disgorge worn hoes, rakes, and wheelbarrows when they're needed. Sometimes I wonder why some of these garden-ers try to grow fig trees in Ontario: they actually dig them up and lay them in trenches before covering them with earth so that the poor trees will have a chance at making it through the winter. What a lot of work! And I've never heard of one actually bearing a good crop of figs.

The North American vernacular garden embraces many influences, as would be expected of a country of recent immi-grants from many lands, yet it bears little resemblance to what might have existed here before the white man arrived. What did exist before? Many native peoples were nomadic hunters and gatherers, but some tribes settled in villages and had gardens. When the explorers and then the pioneers arrived, the Iroquois who lived along the St. Lawrence and around the Great Lakes were already proficient farmers who grew plants for food and medicines, as well as for trade with other tribes. So food was currency as well as sustenance; whether gardening was also ornamental is a moot point. There is some geographical evidence, however, of geometrically patterned ridged fields in what's now Wisconsin, Illinois, and Michigan that date back to the tenth century, suggesting agricultural planting with some attempt at design by a long-ago civilization.

At least we'll have plenty of records of gardens since European settlement to help succeeding generations; information is abundant in contemporary books and gardening magazines, and records of both garden styles and plantings are reasonably plentiful in books written by women pioneers and in historical documents, some kept by Jesuit priests–botanists. The French in particular had quite an influence on the gardens of the New World: for example, the clergy and some settlers who arrived in the seventeenth century brought the potager style of gardening with them. Growing their own vegetables, plus herbs for culinary and medicinal use, was going to be a necessity in this new country, so why not make a pretty garden at the same time? The style became popular, and some potagers were also decorated— with a central ornament such as a sundial, gravel paths, raised beds, and peeled-pole fences; all of them, it could be argued, were practical additions as well. In *Backwoods of Canada,* Catharine Parr Trail describes her early-1800s garden near Peterborough, Ontario, as "in a pretty form; two half circular wings sweep off from the entrance to each side of the house; the fence is a sort of rude basket or hurdle-work, such as you see at home, called by the country folk wattled fence: this forms a much more picturesque fence than those usually put up of split timber." Obviously Catharine also yearned for repose and pleasure in her garden, in the midst of this harsh and unforgiving climate.

Most of the early-ninteenth-century influences in northeastern North American gardens came from England, Scotland,

and Ireland, because that's where most immigrants came from. The Dutch had an early influence in New York (a Dutch colonial settlement named New Amsterdam in the seventeenth century), the French in Louisiana, and the Spanish in the southern and western U.S., with styles that generally included walled or fenced gardens divided by paths and often containing raised beds. Wealthier landowners typically copied the grand estates of their homelands, with belvederes, ponds, and circular driveways cutting graceful arcs through expanses of grass, setting the pattern for North America's love of high-maintenance front lawns. Kitchen gardens ruled for less fortunate folk, but as seed for ornamentals became more available in the new land the urge for growing flowers surfaced. Naturally, seeds came from the old country, either imported or brought in the immigrant's luggage; many grew here happily and some didn't. A few—such as Queen Anne's lace and ox-eye daisies—were so delighted with their new country that they ran away from their gardens to become naturalized field flowers.

Because they'll have advantage of a longer view of history, future garden historians will better understand how social and cultural conditions influenced gardening on this continent, but one influence is already clear: In the nineteenth century, industrialization began to have an effect on urban living conditions, not just in this country but in many countries in the world. Overcrowding and slum conditions were resulting in poor health at best and sickness and deprivation at worst. In Canada, government and business had become convinced by the late nineteenth century that life had to improve for common folk, and this conviction, curiously enough, had an effect on our gardens as well as our public spaces. Municipalities organized the City Beautiful Movement, encouraging the construction of urban recreation areas and parks; gardening became part of the curriculum at schools; horticultural societies formed. The Province of Ontario passed a Public Parks Act in 1883. A decade earlier, the famous (and American) Frederick Law Olmsted, creator of New York's Central Park, designed and built Montreal's Mount Royal Park; in 1904 his former apprentice, Frederick G. Todd, planned Winnipeg's 283-acre Assiniboine Park (it's now 1,100 acres), with curving roads, free-form bodies of water and meadows of grass, English landscape–style. Todd went on to design many more Canadian parks and municipal spaces under the Public Parks Act. The Act to Encourage the Planting and Growing of Trees was passed in 1897. It no doubt is responsible for planting the trees that eventually grew to form arched canopies over the streets of the city of my childhood; they and the beautiful Assiniboine Park, with its lawns and formal beds, its zoo and landmark pavilion, are where my mom, my dad, Bobbie, and I spent many Sunday afternoons, and they're all part of what I remember best about Winnipeg.

Believe it or not, the railway did more than unify the country—it also helped beautify the Canadian countryside and encouraged gardening in concrete ways: growing colourful gardens of annuals around their stations became marks of accomplishment for station agents—who, let's face it, needed something to do between trains in remote areas. Many of these men helped organize the local horticultural societies and foster the interest in gardening in small villages. By the early twentieth century the Canadian Pacific Railway had a forestry department that provided plants for the stations and a horticulturist to offer help to the agents if they needed it. The railway also provided seeds and was instrumental in developing a seed business in Canada—as was the new rage for Victorian bedding, with densely planted gardens that looked like oriental rugs. The station agents favoured familiar annuals—hollyhocks, sweet peas, stocks, petunias, nasturtiums—and later grew old-fashioned perennials like bleeding heart, peonies, and roses, plus shrubs and trees for windbreaks. They generally gardened formal style, with geometric beds and stone pathways; sometimes the name of the town was spelled out in white-painted stones. In 1923 the railway built supply greenhouses in eight areas, and by the '40s ten thousand packets of seeds were sent out annually, plus bedding plants and shrubs. Gardening reached such competitive heights among the agents that the railway awarded annual prizes for the best-looking gardens. Unfortunately, these gardens began to disappear when budgets were cut after the Second World War, but they had already had a significant affect.

English styles influenced gardening in Canada for decades, but at least one gardener as far back as 1918 noted that it might be time to find our own style. "As a nation we are just learning the spirit of gardening as they have it in England," wrote Adele Austen, the chatelaine at Toronto's Spadina House, under the pseudonym Dorothy Perkins in *The Canadian Garden Book;* then she admonished readers to leave formal styles to Europe and to take a homier, more Canadian approach. Her advice might apply today: "Relax! Most of you live in a whirl. Your threadbare, overstrained nerves are crying out for relaxation. Help create a Canadian garden picture!"

But what is Canadian garden style today? People have asked me this question at least half a dozen times, once at a garden seminar in Boston, and I generally fumble for a clear answer. It's not easy to look at your own country and make objective statements. I finally formed a kind of answer, which I will pass on here. How can there be a predominant, identifiable garden style in a nation in which several others could fit, a nation with a huge variety of topographies and climatic zones? The American gardeners attending the Boston seminar understood this sentiment, since their country shares similar conditions, with the added complication of tropical and Mediterranean zones. Yes, there are regional similarities—both in Canada and the U.S.—but the connection is more about plants than garden design. When I think of the gardens of the Prairies a picture comes to mind of beds and borders of bright annuals and gorgeous hardy lilies, which thrive in the long sunny days and cold winters and clearly establish the feeling of Prairie gardens. The same applies to my much-admired dense hedges of southern British Columbia, where mild temperatures and damp weather encourage nearly year-round growth. The rhodos, heathers, and heaths of coastal Nova Scotia prosper in its climate and the acid soil; and in southern Ontario and southern British Columbia we're more apt to see fancy new cultivars than in other parts of the country simply because more nurseries and plant breeders do business in these regions.

Plants that both thrive in a community and are easily available affect the look of its gardens. A line in Eudora Welty's short story "Kin" illustrates my point and will strike a chord with a gardener: "Everybody grew some of the best of everybody else's flowers." We all trade back and forth those plants that do well in our gardens—this was true of Paisley in Ren's time, and it's true of my neighbourhood today. Eudora, by the way, was a dedicated gardener, just as was her mother, Chestina, and their Jackson, Mississippi, garden—considered vernacular because it's characteristic of the style of gardens made from 1925 to '45—is open for tours.

Garden design, however, seems less affected by what region the garden is in than by whether the garden is in the city or the country. The split is urban to rural, not west to east, or north to south. City gardens everywhere tend to be more sophisticated and are usually smaller than country or village gardens, with more precisely pruned shrubs and well-clipped grass. City gardeners also tend to follow prevailing fashion more than do country gardeners: backyards are more planned, with areas for cooking and dining, for sitting, for play. Many urban gardeners express themselves with front-yard gardens of many kinds, formal and casual; sometimes these make a statement, as with native plantings.

Rural gardens, both in the country and in small towns, generally maintain the more structured look of gardens of nearly a century ago, with perimeter borders or island beds of perennials; lilac lanes; vines like clematis, morning glory, or hops growing up a trellis on the front veranda; perhaps a central bed of roses. They're more like the gardens of Paisley than they are like my suburban neighbours' gardens—more "vernacular" than most urban gardens.

But these are rash generalizations, I admit, and one should always be wary of making such statements. The enchanting and practical tiny front vegetable gardens in parts of downtown Toronto may be in the middle of the city, but they fit the strict definition of vernacular better than any other gardens because they share similarities of style and content. I haven't seen many of these in other cities, but maybe I haven't visited the right parts of town. There are more exceptions to my urban/rural generalization—on the television show we featured a spacious and spectacular rural garden in Ontario's Prince Edward County, on Lake Ontario: it had huge rectangular beds filled with modern and antique roses separated with wide pathways, like the best English country gardens; pergolas and arbours offered support for some of the roses and shade for sitting, and the beds displayed large pieces of original and very modern sculpture made by the owner. I visited Douglas Chambers's sophisticated farm garden, a *ferme ornée*, near Walkerton, Ontario—a few miles

MY NATURAL HISTORY

from Paisley's more typical country gardens—where nearly every element held a hidden literary pun or referred in some way to the gardener's or the farm's past; you would need hours and several books of poetry or literary prose to figure out the references, if you had the intellectual wherewithal to do so. The nice thing was that although this garden's layers of meaning existed beyond my knowledge, I didn't feel intimidated: I could enjoy it for its beauty alone. I visited a large vegetable garden laid out in the French *patte d'oise,* or goose-foot, style in Edmonton; and a split-personality suburban garden that combined a red Chinese bridge in a wild front garden of native plants with formal Victorian bedding and classical statuary in the back.

A garden I was taken to in a small Saskatchewan town would fall into the aforementioned category of bizarre. "You must come and see this garden," my hostess insisted. "It's one for the books." Among the roses and the lilies in the tiny backyard cavorted dozens of gnomes and elves in and over a stream fed by a huge mill wheel. I also noticed a Santa in a sleigh and a few reindeer, and a Snow White tucked into the hollow of an old stump, and I'm sure I missed many other characters. I was nonplussed and hardly knew what to say, beyond a polite "How unique! I bet you had fun putting this together!" The gardener was exceedingly proud and clearly pleased that we had come to see his garden.

I also remember with clarity artist Marcia Donohue's jungly urban garden in Berkeley, California, visited as part of *Canadian Gardening*'s 1997 tour. She had a forty-foot-tall blue-bottle tree, and I mean that literally: the ends of its limbs sported cobalt-blue bottles that glowed in the sunshine like exotic tube-shaped flowers. She also had bowling balls "growing" among the begonias, with old silver spoons standing up beside them, and flowered plates glued to three-foot-tall poles of rebar blooming

191

among the hollyhocks. It was a wonderful, wacky garden, with lots of real plants, too. "I love it when people leave here and feel they can go home and do whatever they want in their gardens because they see I'm doing what I want to do," Marcia said.

These may be considered "art" gardens as much as vernacular gardens, although I think they fall into the vernacular category because they were made by gardeners expressing themselves and not trying to create grand garden design. They were made for the gardeners' own pleasure, from their own imaginations and by their own hands, with no help from designers. Their own talents and interests provided the design direction.

Fifty years from now, maybe some garden historian will be able to definitively answer that question I've been asked so often, and I wish I could be around to hear the response. Maybe by then there will be an identifiable Canadian garden style, but I rather hope it's not one that's too rigidly recognizable. We all need to be ourselves in the garden. Assuming we haven't annihilated the world or the human race by then, I hope we will have reached the point where all gardeners have discovered the rewards of creating their own particular styles and have the confidence not to copy others. I hope each gardener has reached a satisfactory point of attainment with his or her garden so that it offers pleasure and repose while it also accords with nature, helps fight off personal demons, and takes its owner back to a happy place from childhood.

CHAPTER 14

Gardening

IN THE MOMENT

· · · · ·

P EGGY LEE'S "Is That All There Is?" was my theme song for a while, because to me it was about the search for the grown-up time, when everything is finally in place and you are happy, but then you really grow up and realize this state of affairs will never come to pass. You face reality. Life never comes wrapped in a glittery package and tied with a shiny bow.

For those of you unfamiliar with the song, it's a haunting spoken-and-sung number in which Miss Peggy Lee describes a number of life's experiences—watching her house burn down, going to the circus, falling in love—and after each she feels that something is missing. She asks the title's question, sung as the chorus: *Is that all there is?*

In the last verse she anticipates her listener's question: Well, then, what's the point? Why not just end it all now? She says she's not ready for that final disappointment. She'll always be asking *Is that all there is?*

I find this song positive because it recognizes that life never ties things into neat, satisfying packages; in fact, the end will almost always seem to come too soon, but I've heard others say it's a sad song about disappointment and disillusionment, about a jaded person who will never be satisfied. I prefer my take—I think it's more optimistic—but let's address the subject at hand: the garden, which in an existential sense relates to the song.

Sooner or later all gardeners have to face the fact that their garden has it own stubborn existence and that the desired point of attainment Gertrude Jekyll spoke about, the one you are trying to impose on your garden, will always elude you even if you sip from the fountain of youth and are awarded another hundred years to spend trying. It takes too many gardeners too long to realize that to be happy with their gardens they have to live in the moment. If they don't, they will always be asking themselves *Is that all there is?*

This is particularly true of the down seasons. You have to appreciate the darkest times of the year, to be able to look out one cold, blustery November day and really see that the dead brown leaves scattered over the pathway and hugging the dead stems of the perennials have a decadent beauty; it may be different from their fresh spring beauty, when they announce their youth in shades of chartreuse and kelly and a step further along in the life process from their glorious fall colours, but the scene's subtlety can give you pleasure just the same. The network of dark twigs high in the Norway maple, moving hypnotically in the wind against the Prussian blue sky, is something you don't see at all in summer because the twigs are fully clothed; late fall is the time to appreciate the tree's true form and perhaps be happy it's there in your garden. And you may want to pick up a paintbrush when you truly drink in the November colours of the dried tawny flowers of the now-past-it hydrangea bush against the greyed texture of the neighbour's weathered woodshed.

Living in the moment applies to other seasons, too. At first gardeners long for summer because it's the best season, then one busy spring day, when it seems as though the garden is nothing but work and you're slogging about in the beds and borders preparing them for the main event, which will pass as quickly as Christmas does to a child, you come across the jack-in-the-pulpit you'd forgotten you planted in the side garden, hiding under its three-part leaves. Wow! What a happy surprise! Its otherworldly bloom makes a brief appearance—all the more reason to love it while it exists—and without fanfare in brown and green. Then you have a greater surprise in fall when you discover its cluster of brilliant red berries.

The same appreciation must be given to plants you've grown heartily sick of, like the shocking pink rhododendron I fell victim to at a nursery one dank spring day years ago when buying plants for the front garden. It blooms like a neon light in early May, attracting favourable comments from passersby who don't have to look at it every day. It's one smart little shrub, too: it fades quickly just as I've had a bellyful, ensuring it will have another season of life. But I've learned to respect the vitality that rhodo brings to the garden in spring and actually welcome it with open arms—as long as it doesn't stay too long.

Time is an important element in any garden. At first I wondered if the bergenia, my grandma's old pig squeak, would ever fill the space allotted for it, and before you knew it I was pulling out bits and begging the neighbours to take some. One of the apple trees that were part of the reason we bought the house in the first place fell over in a rainstorm, taking with it the sweet autumn clematis clinging to its trunk and a few apples ripening on its branches. It left a serious void in the front garden, and we sorely felt its absence. Now the void is filled with a purple smoke tree, and I can hardly remember the apple tree.

And so it goes. Nature herself has as much control over the garden as does the gardener, perhaps more, and never is this fact more apparent than with the weather. A decade ago, after a long, cloudy, and cold spring, I finally learned to let the weather have its way—you can't do much else, anyway. The bulbs took forever to show their stubby little noses, and then they'd retreat back into the earth when the mercury dipped below frigid, making me fear they'd never again see the light of day. The perennials sulked under the frozen surface, and the apple trees missed their blooming date by at least a week. I got chillblains when I ventured into the garden, so I mainly stayed inside. Then when the weather warmed up I had two weeks to do a month's chores.

Suddenly, answering the call of a warming sun and a new season, the bulbs broke the surface of the earth. Because the temperatures stayed cool, the blooms lasted for weeks longer than usual—the crocuses overlapped the daffodils; the daffodils tumbled over the tulips; the tulips jammed up against the grape hyacinths and grew taller than they had for years. The alliums seemed to last all summer. The apple trees had more blossoms, and they hung on longer than they had since we'd moved in. Best of all, it was a great spring to divide and move perennials: in the cool soil and dull days transplant shock was nonexistent.

That long, cool, and finally flower-filled spring led to a summer garden rich with bloom, I'm sure because the plants had time to develop sturdy roots and strong constitutions before the sun and heat encouraged top growth.

The garden is not the place for control freaks and perfectionists, and yet I know that in my callow youth I tried to make mine conform. I used to wish for the time when it would be finished, when it would reach the perfection I envisioned. Now I know it's going to be different every year, and I will have had less to do with how it looks than I'd hoped, beyond setting out the basic plan and guiding and maintaining the plants. That chilly spring followed by a gorgeous summer garden was another epiphany for me—I learned not to complain about nature's caprices but to let the tide take me and to keep my head above the waves.

I also realized I wasn't alone in coming to this plateau of understanding. Gardeners who'd been through many springs and summers of both good and bad weather seemed naturally to reach some kind of understanding with their gardens. And as I met more gardeners through the magazine and television show, I realized we shared other stages of development, too. These people were like me and I like them; we liked to think we're artists with trowels instead of brushes and paints, doing exciting and different things in our gardens, but generally we're a pretty predictable lot who approach gardening in similar ways.

And so I developed a theory of the stages of gardening, which I present to you forthwith. Who knows—they may even be integral elements in our green fingers.

THE SIX STAGES OF GARDENING

1. *I Want it All, Now*

In the beginning, gardeners want colour, as much of it as possible all season long. We're hungry for the big hit—that's the goal of making a garden, right? This means annuals, which knock themselves out trying to please us for one glorious summer. This stage may last a year or two, sometimes longer. We move on to Stage 2 when our beds are all beginning to look a bit much and we realize replacing the garden every year is expensive.

197

2. *Discovering a Love that Lasts*

We settle down a bit and begin to appreciate perennials, which have more subtle colour ranges. Perennials live longer but have shorter blooming periods, sometimes as little as a week, which means gardening is more challenging and demands good planning for continuous bloom. Gardening with perennials is like conducting a symphony orchestra and just as satisfying. This stage can last a few years because it's a learning process.

3. *Going for the Green*
Next up—foliage and texture, the green stuff. Suddenly we notice that leaves come in interesting shades of green, sometimes in greys or lovely deep shades of purple, and in many textures— feathery and ferny, leathery and quilted. This stage can overlap with Stage 2. We become more sophisticated in our tastes and more demanding of our plantings, but towards the end of this stage we feel vaguely discontented. The garden looks disconnected. There's no structure, no shape.

4. *Gardening by Design*
What we need is a plan. The most admired gardens in the world are as notable for their "bones" as their plants—Vita Sackville-West's Sissinghurst in Kent, Rosemary Verey's Barnsley House in Gloucestershire, Frank Cabot's Les Quatre Vents in Quebec, to name a few. We see that a plan is the essence of a garden, its personality, what makes it endure. Without a plan, a garden is a jumble of plants. In this stage we hire some design help, we take some courses, or we read more garden design books.

5. *Barking Up the Right Trees*

We learn to see, really see, trees and shrubs, their shapes, and the way they give the garden background and carry it through the winter with their strong presence. It's too bad this stage couldn't have come first, since trees and shrubs take so long to become established and fitting them into an existing garden is so difficult. But we muddle through, working with what we have and replacing where we can. Appreciating bark and its various textures and colours is also part of this stage.

6. *The Winter of Our Content*

At last, we learn to love winter, and not only because it brings a rest from summer's chores. We admire its subtle browns and bronzes, its deep maroons and shades of grey and black. Its shapes, too—skeleton trees and bare, twisting vines. The way the sun glancing through the arbour casts shadow patterns on the path for a fleeting midday moment. We realize that the garden's changes are good, that winter can have as much beauty as any season, and we learn to go with the flow.

Come to think of it, these stages echo the stages in our lives, from the desire for immediate gratification in our youth to the deeper and mellower pleasures of maturity. But don't assume that I've learned how to live in the moment just because I've lived a few years in my garden and have learned to appreciate its changes; I think living in the moment is a goal we may not reach until it's almost too late. If ever. But I'm getting there.

My first eye-opening revelation happened twenty years ago and was one of those epiphanies that becomes a turning point in life. My memory plays it as a seminal moment, a curtain suddenly drawn back to let in a ray of brilliant sun, but I know it was really an ordinary moment. The difference is that I was ready to accept the message.

The message was delivered by another young man, a friend of Joe's bringing a package for him. I was sitting by the pond in the backyard with my foot propped up on cushions, nursing a badly broken ankle held together with metal pins, and working on copy that the magazine had couriered to me. I was unable to go to the office; I was unable to put even an ounce of weight on my healing bone, unable to walk without crutches, unable to putter in the garden. I was miserable.

"Wow, what a great garden!" said the young man, dropping the package and hunkering down beside me. "What a lucky duck you are to be able to do your work out here!"

"Oh, *really?*" I said in my newly adopted tone of sardonic forbearance. Then I launched into my litany of complaints: having to crutch out the portable phone, my lunch, my water bottle, and my magazine work in my backpack every morning took a lot of effort, and I had to keep holding my papers down or they'd blow away. I needed a port-a-potty because getting back to the house to use the bathroom was a real pain. Sure I could look at the garden, but the weeds were taking over, the flowers needed deadheading, everything including my ankle was falling apart. . .

The young man looked puzzled. "But this garden is better than any office," he said. "Think of the time you're saving by not having to drive into the middle of the city and go to all those meetings. Listen to the birds. . . look at those flowers. . . I bet you never get a chance to sit out here and enjoy them. What an opportunity to just sit and think!"

I stopped mid-sentence, my mouth open. This young man, not a whole lot older than some of the shoes in my closet, had a good point. Here was my chance to read those books I'd set aside for a vacation; here was the perfect opportunity to catch up on my recipe file, to gaze at the garden in the changing light of the afternoon and plan its future. Here was time for all sorts of sedentary pastimes I'd complained I couldn't fit into my busy schedule.

I have had other revealing moments, of course, such as the jack-in-the-pulpit moment in the side garden, and the sleepy summer dawn when I glanced out the kitchen window while making coffee and my eye caught a fleeting ray of sun shining through the goat's beard and turning its creamy blossoms into molten gold. But this young man holds the record for providing the seminal moment—he helped me realize that life, as well as gardening, is indeed a journey with many worthwhile stops along the way, if you'd only you take your eyes off the road long enough to recognize them. And if you do, you'll never have to ask if that's all there is.

·　·　·　·　·

WISH I'D KEPT a better photographic record of our garden over the years, and by better I mean something more than the snapshots I take three or four times a season to remind myself where the holes are in the spring bulb display or where the garden could benefit from fall colour.

My ideal is a time-lapse film that covers a few years, with a frame recorded every few days from exactly the same vantage point. Finished and edited, it would unfold like a movie and would reveal more than the growth and change in our garden. It might tell us something about nature, interesting tidbits like how many days it takes for those libidinous little red beetles to defoliate a lily to how many monarch butterflies an agastache plant can hold at one time without bending. Those little moments would be filmed separately as close-up vignettes and edited in —B-roll, they call it in the TV world—and would offer a welcome change of view and add a personal touch to the story of the garden. Maybe other people might even like to see it. With the right voiceover and music do you think there's any possibility it could work as a science documentary?

Who knows—a time-lapse record just of our front garden might actually be worth watching because it's changed so much on its own over its twelve years. It started out more or less as

I'd imagined it: three large areas divided by a narrow Y-shaped gravel path, a few shrubs on the property line, and the three areas filled with tapestries of low plants, some, such as the bergenia and thymes, with foliage that remains all winter. I got the tapestry idea from a garden book, and the word was so evocative that it helped me choose plants in blending shades and mounding shapes that would weave together. But I woke up a couple of summers ago to the sudden realization that it had become a different garden while I wasn't looking—proof of how time and its owners' inattention can affect a garden.

It's well behaved enough in spring, with many clumps of crocuses and tulips, the pasqueflower that reminds me of the crocus I used to see on the prairies, plus pink, mauve, and purple moss phlox, aubrieta, and other low-flowering plants welcoming the new season. A neighbour across the road tells me she always has her coffee by her front window in spring so that she can enjoy our garden. Then a row of slightly taller The Fairy roses begins its pretty pink bloom, along with a grouping of lavender, rosy prairie smoke, blue catmint growing against chartreuse cushion euphorbia, and lady's mantle, and that rather raucous (and taller) pink rhodo, toned down with a couple of lower mauve ones at its base. Grey lamb's ears, bergenia, Jack Frost brunnera, and blue fescue maintain the pattern of moderate height and balance the flower colours.

But in high summer another personality emerges. Muscular interlopers have moved aside the dwarf astilbe, the campanulas, and the low veronica and are taking over—plants like purple coneflower; shasta daisies; purple and sickly mauve asters; yellow evening primrose; blue agastache; a couple of butterfly bushes; Joe-Pye weed; mullein; and the dreaded creeping snow-in-summer, which wreaks havoc with the thymes and is almost impossible to eradicate. Oh, it's pretty enough, with its white blooms and small grey foliage, but it's another garden thug. A couple of lilies have also sprung up, bringing those constantly copulating red lily beetles with them.

I didn't put in any of these interlopers; they migrated from their place in the back garden—except for the mullein, snow-in-summer, and Joe-Pye weed, which came from outer space. I presume the birds brought the others to the front, where they're thriving in the warm western exposure; unfortunately most are so happy there they're hitting three or four feet in height and make the garden look like a poor man's Henri Rousseau painting. Soon the garden police will be calling.

I suppose I should be flattered that these plants like our front garden so much they insist on staying and proliferating, but I'm regretfully encouraging them to move on. A couple of summers ago we started to dig them out (I've given most of them away to other gardeners) and replace them with lower-growing varieties—a big swath of salvias, a few more low grasses, some blue leadwort. And I'm keeping watch from now on. But I wonder how a time-lapse film would turn out if I left the garden alone and the camera kept recording frames for the next century. Would the garden revert to its origins? A century ago our property was part of an orchard; before that it was boreal forest; millennia ago it was under the waters of the ancient Lake Iroquois.

I expect our garden would never get back in time even as far as the orchard—long before then it will become part of the provincial highway that runs near our house or the location of a dozen new townhouses. Now, that would be a lesson on a DVD.

I do wish I'd thought to keep a better record of the garden that I could put on a CD to pass along to my children. I'd like to have a CD of Uncle Ren's garden, too, but all I have is what I remember. I'm not even sure my kids—adults now, almost as old as their mother, in fact—have all inherited the family's green fingers or would even care to have a record of my garden. The work ethic seems to be ruling for now. Suzy has an impressive front rock garden and a nice back perennial bed but little time to tend it. Michael regularly fries hanging baskets of plants outside his south-facing apartment window in summer, but he often has a vase of fresh flowers in his living room, so maybe there's hope there.

Joe showed some early promise as a grower of herbs, if you get my drift. One March when he was a teenager his funny-looking tomatoes sprouted mysteriously alongside mine on a basement windowsill, in little peat pots he'd borrowed from my shelf of garden supplies. I pretended I hadn't noticed, and I monitored their progress, and the little seedlings just as mysteriously disappeared in May, reappearing under the Siberian elm hedge. Then they disappeared altogether. I thought they'd died for lack of sunshine, and I didn't get around to asking him what had happened to them until a couple of years ago. He didn't know either, but he suspected that one of his buddies had harvested the crop, all five four-inch plants. I guess that failure discouraged him from future gardening practice, although today he does have a lush, chest-high rosemary plant on his patio in southern California that I lust after. So he must have some green fingers, if not the space to exercise them.

Matthew has ten green fingers, maybe more. He also has an artistic eye and has designed some beautiful beds and borders, and he knows how to do practical things like build a pool surround using a rubber mould that makes poured concrete look like genuine stone, right down to the natural variations in colour. But I'm particularly envious of his skill as a grower. He's much more meticulous than I am, and he gets better results from his plants.

His teenage son, Kyle, my oldest grandson, is the one who may hit the gardening annals (the other two, both younger than

205

Kyle, are too busy with hockey and dance). Kyle's not involved with ornamentals as yet, but he's had a vegetable garden almost every summer since he was four (he's seventeen as I write this), and last year he grew tomatoes, broccoli, beets, eggplant, and more, from seed started indoors under lights. This year, fulfilling the role of a new gardener, he has plans to grow only unusual varieties—ones you're not likely to see in the average vegetable garden.

I expect Uncle Ren has his eye on him.

ACKNOWLEDGMENTS

WISH I COULD THANK everyone who's had a hand in helping me write this book. Here are some of them: Don Sedgwick and Shaun Bradley of Transatlantic Literary Agency: Don for convincing me that I really did have something to say and Shaun for asking that important first question; Rob Sanders and Nancy Flight of Greystone Books for their enthusiasm and downright niceness—it's good to hear someone say they love your writing; My husband, Chris Zelkovich, for letting me bounce ideas off him and lean on him when I needed to; Lou Challinor for reading the first draft and offering comments based on many years of friendship; Karen Hanley for reading the first draft and making suggestions as both a dear friend and a fellow editor who's always been on my wavelength. Only she and I will ever know which words are hers; Dr. Jim Alcock for helping me find the right psychology books; Professor Deborah McLennan for her professional advice, delivered with a sense of humour; Susan Folkins for being the consummate editor: sensitive, supportive, and objective; Iva Cheung for her professional and therefore invisible copy editing; and my kids for saying they'd still love me no matter what I wrote about them.